3/18 Cavendish 33⁰⁰

CULTURES OF THE WORLD
Liberia

Cavendish
Square

New York

Published in 2018 by Cavendish Square Publishing, LLC
243 5th Avenue, Suite 136, New York, NY 10016
Copyright © 2018 by Cavendish Square Publishing, LLC

Third Edition

This publication represents the opinions and views of the author based on his or her personal experience, knowledge, and research. The information in this book serves as a general guide only. The author and publisher have used their best efforts in preparing this book and disclaim liability rising directly or indirectly from the use and application of this book.
All websites were available and accurate when this book was sent to press.

Library of Congress Cataloging-in-Publication Data

Names: Levy, Patricia, 1951- author. | Spilling, Michael, author. | Griffin, Brett, author.
Title: Liberia / Patricia Levy, Michael Spilling, and Brett Griffin.
Description: New York : Cavendish Square Publishing, 2018. | Series: Cultures of the world (third edition) | Includes bibliographical references and index. | Audience: Grades 5-8.
Identifiers: LCCN 2017046636 (print) | LCCN 2017047199 (ebook) | ISBN 9781502636263 (library bound) | ISBN 9781502636270 (eBook) Subjects: LCSH: Liberia--Juvenile literature.
Classification: LCC DT624 (ebook) | LCC DT624 .L47 2017 (print) | DDC 966.62--dc23
LC record available at https://lccn.loc.gov/2017046636

Editorial Director: David McNamara
Editor: Kristen Susienka
Copy Editor: Nathan Heidelberger
Associate Art Director: Amy Greenan
Designer: Alan Sliwinski
Production Coordinator: Karol Szymczuk
Photo Research: J8 Media

PICTURE CREDITS

Printed in the United States of America

CONTENTS

LIBERIA TODAY

LOCATED ON THE WEST COAST OF AFRICA, LIBERIA IS THE OLDEST independent republic on the continent. Founded by freed slaves from the United States and the Caribbean in the early nineteenth century, Liberia is unique for having escaped the colonization and imperialism that have defined much of the modern history of virtually every other African nation. That does not mean that Liberia has not seen its share of challenges, however. Since its very inception, an ethnic divide has existed between the descendants of the former slaves who settled the country, known as Americo-Liberians, and the country's indigenous tribes. For most of Liberia's history, the minority Americo-Liberian community held total control over the country's government and denied basic rights to the majority of the population. Despite attempts at reform, this tension exploded in 1980 with a military coup that toppled the Americo-Liberian government. A military dictatorship ensued, which in turn led to a civil war that raged from 1989 until 2003.

Though peace has since returned to the country, the government (now representative of the entire population) faces the daunting task of rebuilding most of the nation's infrastructure from scratch. Political stability has been restored, but the trust of the Liberian people has been slower to recover—after more than two decades of unresponsive or absent government, an entire generation of citizens has come of age with a reflexive skepticism of its elected officials. The government has set about rejuvenating the country's shattered economy and making much-needed improvements to the country's damaged transportation network, health-care system, and sanitation infrastructure, but for the Liberian citizenry, much work still needs to be done.

Liberians are a diverse people, from dozens of ethnic, linguistic, and religious backgrounds, united by the overwhelming poverty that characterizes the country. Liberia is among the poorest nations on the planet, and most Liberians live on less than one US dollar a day. Finding food and clean water is a daily struggle, and the country's sanitation system is still in poor condition more than a decade after the cease-fire. This contributes heavily to the spread of disease, which the Liberian health-care system is in no condition to effectively combat—an Ebola epidemic in 2014 burned through the country, killing almost five thousand Liberians before international agencies

Rural Liberians often walk long distances to collect water for their family's use.

successfully brought it under control. The country's schools are understaffed and underfunded, and many Liberian children lack the means or opportunity to attend; even if they do, less than 10 percent of the country has access to electricity or the internet, making it difficult to continue studies outside of the classroom. Finally, Liberia's environment is already feeling the effects of climate change, and rapid deforestation has done tremendous damage to both the traditional lifestyle of the country's rural inhabitants and the habitats of the exotic wildlife that calls the rain forest home.

Facing these problems, the Liberian people persevere. In the capital city of Monrovia, the few nightclubs that receive electricity attract a regular clientele, and there is a burgeoning art scene growing in the city's crowded streets. In the countryside, rural Liberians come together for a variety of traditional festivals and tribal ceremonies. And in the halls of power, Liberia continues to be unique among its neighbors.

The country's first democratic elections in more than twenty-five years were held in 2005, and Ellen Johnson Sirleaf won the presidency. Of indigenous Liberian ancestry, Johnson Sirleaf became the first female elected head of state in the history of the African continent and was a recipient of the Nobel Peace Prize in 2011. Johnson Sirleaf's administration has had success in returning some degree of political and economic stability to the country, and though Liberia still has a very long way to go, the nation and its people look with hope and resolve to the future.

GEOGRAPHY

The Atlantic Ocean washes the Liberian coastline in Robertsport.

L IBERIA IS LOCATED ON THE WEST coast of Africa, a few degrees north of the equator. It shares a border with three other African nations: Sierra Leone to the northwest, Guinea to the north, and the Ivory Coast to the east. To the south and west, Liberia borders the Atlantic Ocean.

The land in Liberia is divided among coastal lowlands, plateaus, and highlands. Most of the land located inland from the coastal strip is covered by tropical rain forest. Despite the threat of deforestation, Liberia still boasts 44.5 percent of all the rain forest in West Africa.

Despite years of civil war and the recent Ebola epidemic, the population of Liberia continues to grow, with 2016 estimates putting it around 4.3 million. The Liberian people are evenly divided between urban and rural settings, though the population density of the biggest cities is high. More than one-quarter of Liberia's entire population—1.3 million people—lives in the capital city, Monrovia, which has led to difficulties in ensuring that all of these residents have access to clean water, sanitation services, health care, and other basic needs.

RIVERS AND THE COAST

Liberia contains many rivers, some of which act as natural barriers between the country and its neighbors. These rivers have in turn come to define Liberia's borders. The Mano rises in the Guinea

Highlands, northeast of the city of Voinjama, and forms more than 90 miles (145 kilometers) of the Liberia—Sierra Leone border. In the east, the Cavalla originates north of the Nimba Mountains in Guinea and flows south, forming the majority of the border between Liberia and the Ivory Coast. Liberia's border with Guinea is also partly determined by the course of a river, in this case the Saint Paul.

Liberia's rivers are important sources of water for agricultural land in the interior of the country, as well as natural power sources. In 2016, the country generated 36.7 percent of its electricity from hydroelectric plants. Hydroelectric energy has been generated from both the Saint Paul River and the Farmington River, a tributary of the larger Lofa River. Though the hydropower-generating stations were destroyed in the civil war, the Mount Coffee hydropower plant, which draws from the Saint Paul River, underwent extensive modernization and was reopened in December 2016. The plant is eventually expected to generate electricity for more than one hundred thousand Liberians.

While Liberia's rivers provide irrigation and electric power to the country, they are poorly suited to transportation. Most of the country's rivers contain several stretches of rapids and waterfalls, as well as large rocky deposits near the coast. Seasonal rainfall and the rapid runoff which follows can also wreak havoc with water levels, making navigation of the country's rivers all but impossible in places. The Saint Paul, for example, is only navigable for 18 miles (29 km) upstream from the coast, while the river itself flows for 280 miles (450 km) from source to sea.

Liberia's coastline is marked by numerous estuaries, partially enclosed bodies of water in which the country's rivers meet the sea. Wave action has also caused long sandbars to form along the coastline, creating a series of shallow lagoons between the shore and the open ocean. The coastline is further characterized by mangrove swamps, trees, and shrubs that grow in saline coastal habitats throughout the tropics. Between the shifting sandbars and the rocky deposits left by rivers joining the sea, Liberia contains no natural harbors. Despite this fact, the fertility of the coastline has prompted numerous settlements to grow up along it, and the country's largest cities—Monrovia, Marshall, and Buchanan, among others—are all on the coast.

The Mount Coffee hydropower plant derives electricity from the Saint Paul River.

PLATEAUS AND HIGHLANDS

Plateaus are areas of high and level ground, and they are abundant in Liberia. Gradually rising from a series of rolling hills and foothills, the plateaus have an average height of approximately 1,000 feet (305 meters), with those farthest

THE LOFA RIVER

The Lofa River, which has its source in the country of Guinea, flows from northeast to southwest before reaching its mouth in the Atlantic Ocean. It traverses the entire width of Liberia in the process.

Liberia lies on the Atlantic coast of West Africa and borders three other African states.

inland reaching heights of 1,500 feet (457 m) or more. Some parts of the plateaus remain relatively unexplored because of both the dense, impenetrable rain forest and the unnavigable rivers in the interior of the country. Parts of the hilly country, on the other hand, are home to many of Liberia's biggest coffee plantations, and were among the first places in the country to be mined for iron ore.

Liberia's highlands rise to about 4,000 feet (1,219 m) above sea level and spread across all of Liberia's borders. In the northeast, they cross over into Guinea, where they form the foothills of the Guinea Highlands. Farther east, they include the Nimba Mountains, which continue into the Ivory Coast and Guinea; Mount Nimba at Guest House Hill (5,748 feet/1,752 m) straddles the borders of the Ivory Coast, Guinea, and Liberia. At the western end of these highlands are the Wologizi Mountains, close to Sierra Leone. Not surprisingly, the mountainous regions are the least developed and least populated parts of the country.

THE CLIMATE

As a result of its location just north of the equator, daily temperatures in Liberia range from 79 to 90 degrees Fahrenheit (26 to 32 degrees Celsius). Combined

HIGHEST PEAKS

The highest peak located entirely within the country of Liberia is Mount Wuteve in the north, which reaches a height of 4,747 feet (1,447 meters). Though Mount Nimba is taller, only part of that mountain is in Liberia.

with a relative humidity that averages 88 percent, on most days the country is extremely hot and sticky.

One of the few respites from the high humidity of this equatorial climate comes at the end of the year, when the dust-laden desert winds known as the harmattan blow from the Sahara region toward western Liberia. This dry season has been lengthened by almost a month in recent years, due to deforestation and drought in the Sahel—a vast semidesert region north of Liberia. During the dry season (between December and April), days are hot, but not unpleasantly so, and nights are comfortably cool. There is also usually a brief period that resembles the dry season around July or August.

By contrast, the rainy season, which stretches from May to November, sees the relative humidity climb to as high as 95 percent. There is heavy rainfall along the coast at this time, since it is there that the rainy season begins earliest; Cape Mount records as much as 205 inches (521 centimeters) of rainfall every year. Across the country, rain usually falls in long and heavy

Mount Nimba towers over the borders of Liberia, Guinea, and the Ivory Coast.

LIBERIA'S BORDERS, BY THE NUMBERS

Total area: 43,000 square miles (111,370 square kilometers)—slightly larger than the US state of Tennessee
Coast measure: 360 miles (579 km)
Land boundaries: 1,036 miles (1,667 km)—shared with Guinea for 367 miles (590 km), the Ivory Coast for 483 miles (778 km), and Sierra Leone for 186 miles (299 km)

MONROVIA

The capital city of Liberia, Monrovia, was founded in 1822 on the left bank of the Saint Paul River, on the ridge formed by Cape Mesurado. The city is spread across an area divided into a number of small islands by lagoons. It offers a panoramic view of the Atlantic Ocean and the coastal plains.

Monrovia and its suburbs occupy 5 square miles (13 sq km). The layout of the city reflects the North American origins of the first settlers who designed Monrovia, and some of the older buildings are reminiscent of the architecture of the southern United States. The city's design, however, has become a problem in recent years. Originally intended to support ten thousand citizens, Monrovia is now home to 1.3 million Liberians, and its infrastructure has become overwhelmed. The city's narrow streets are extremely difficult for vehicles to navigate; the roads are in poor condition; and many Monrovians still lack access to electricity, clean water, and health care.

The main port and center of industrial activity is on Bushrod Island, which benefits from a deepwater harbor that was constructed as an American military base between 1944 and 1948. In addition to the main wharf where large ships can load and unload, there are also specially built piers for shipping iron ore. Roberts International Airport, Liberia's primary airport, is located 35 miles (56 km) from Monrovia.

The population of Monrovia is cosmopolitan and includes all of the country's ethnic groups, as well as refugees, other Africans, Lebanese, and other Asians and Europeans.

downpours that may last from a few hours to two or three days. In the interior, the average annual rainfall is about half that of the coastal regions. The relative humidity is also lower away from the coast.

ANIMAL LIFE

Liberia is home to 193 species of mammals, including leopards, monkeys, chimpanzees, antelopes, elephants, and anteaters.

Two of Liberia's rarest mammals are the manatee and the pygmy hippopotamus. Manatees are aquatic herbivorous mammals. They have been overhunted for their meat. The West African species of manatee, *Trichechus senegalensis*, is far less common than it once was. Hippopotami are some of the largest land mammals, but the pygmy hippopotamus, *Hexaprotodon liberiensis*, is a modest 5 to 6 feet (1.5 to 1.8 m) tall. It is found only in the wilds of West Africa. Pygmy hippos are solitary and secretive animals, and they spend much more time out of the water than their larger cousins. Foraging for food in the forests, they run for the protection of streams or rivers only in times of danger.

The rain forest environment and the coastal habitat support a rich variety of bird, reptile, and insect life. Parrots, hornbills, and woodpeckers are common in the forests, and along the coast flamingos search for small

The city of Monrovia was named after James Monroe, the fifth president of the United States, making Liberia the only country (other than the United States itself) whose capital is named for an American president.

The pygmy hippopotamus is a rare mammal native to West Africa.

animals and algae in the muddy waters of the lagoons. Also found in the rain forest are scorpions, lizards, at least eight varieties of poisonous snakes, and many unusual birds and bats. Three types of crocodile live along the banks of Liberia's rivers.

The political instability that plagued Liberia from 1989 to 2003 resulted in poor control over poaching, and this contributed to the growing number of animal species that continue to face extinction. Food insecurity has forced many Liberians to turn to bushmeat for sustenance, as they face a choice between hunting wild animals in the rain forest or starving. Deforestation has also contributed to the dwindling numbers of wildlife. Ecosystems are disrupted and habitats are destroyed with every acre of rain forest that is cleared.

FLORA

The diverse array of animal species in Liberia is matched by the wide variety of plant life in the country. Liberia's flora—particularly its trees—is also incredibly important to the economy. Of particular significance is the rubber tree. Growing up to 130 feet (40 m) tall, these trees yield a milky white fluid called latex, from which rubber is produced. Early in the twentieth century, a British-German company began to produce rubber for export from wild

RUBBER PRODUCTION

Latex is collected by cutting into the bark of the rubber tree and collecting the flow in a small cup. Each cut yields only a tablespoonful of latex, but a new cut can be made every other day. The trees are then periodically left to renew themselves. When a sufficient amount of latex has been collected, it is mixed with water and acid to help the particles of rubber adhere to one another. This allows the rubber to be compressed by a machine, and the sheets of rubber that emerge from the machine's rollers are then dried.

rubber trees in Liberia. It was not long before a plantation was created and thousands of rubber trees were planted. The first plantation was eventually forced to close down because of falling world rubber prices, but when the market improved in the mid-1920s, the Firestone Tire and Rubber Company acquired the plantation and expanded it to about 1 million acres (405,000 hectares).

The Liberian rain forest is home to a wide variety of plant and animal life.

Another economically important tree is the coffee tree, and more than one species flourishes in Liberia. Until Brazil began to dominate the market in the late nineteenth century, Liberia's economy was bolstered by the export of coffee from the indigenous species *Coffea liberica*. This species is still cultivated in the coastal region, but it produces an inferior type of coffee that has a bitter taste. In the north of the country, the imported species *Coffea robusta*, which is largely used in the manufacture of instant coffee, is far more common.

The kola tree, native to tropical Africa, is also found in Liberia. It is popular for its nuts, which provide a source of caffeine when chewed. There is a small export trade of kola nuts to Guinea.

INTERNET LINKS

http://www.worldatlas.com/webimage/countrys/africa/lr.htm
The World Atlas includes maps of Liberia, as well as information about the country's geography, history, and important figures.

https://www.worldtravelguide.net/guides/africa/liberia
The guide to Liberia contained here gives background information about the country to prospective travelers, as well as details about the nation's climate and the best times of year in which to visit.

HISTORY

The first president of Liberia lived in an executive mansion (pictured here) modeled on the architecture of the American South, from where many Liberians emigrated.

2

FOUNDED IN 1822, LIBERIA IS THE oldest independent country in Africa. Originally intended by American philanthropic organizations as a homeland for former slaves, between 1822 and 1867 approximately nineteen thousand people were "returned" to Africa. Most of this number had never lived in Africa, however, having been born as slaves or free blacks in the United States, and they therefore brought a distinctly different culture with them to Africa.

In many cases, the new arrivals shared almost nothing in common with the local tribes that were native to the region from which Liberia was formed. The "repatriated" Americans and Africans nevertheless took charge of the new settlement, beginning a cultural and class divide that persists to the present day.

Until 1980, Liberia was governed exclusively by Americo-Liberians, the descendants of those original settlers who came to Africa from the United States and the Caribbean. Though they comprised only a tiny minority of the overall population (about 5 percent), Americo-Liberians held virtually every position of power in the country and benefited from a higher standard of living than the indigenous population. This ethnic and class divide eventually contributed to a military coup in 1980, which

"We, the people of the Republic of Liberia, were originally inhabitants of the United States of North America. In some parts of that country we were debarred by law from all rights and privileges of man ... We uttered our complaints, but they were unattended to, or only met by alleging the peculiar institutions of the country."
—Liberian Declaration of Independence, 1847

in turn precipitated a fourteen-year civil war in which hundreds of thousands of Liberians lost their lives. Though peace was restored in 2003 and democratic elections were held in 2005, Liberia still has a long way to go to heal its divides. The years since the end of the civil war have seen the country make significant strides in restoring democracy and political stability, but the government has had less success in providing basic goods and services to the Liberian people. Food, water, sanitation, health care, and electricity are still luxuries in Liberia, and the country remains extremely poor. These challenges were exacerbated by an epidemic of the Ebola virus that broke out in 2014 and cost nearly five thousand Liberian lives. The country is now Ebola-free, but the long-term effects of the disease are still being felt, adding further strain to Liberia's already overwhelmed institutions and presenting even more obstacles to be overcome if the country is to address the many pressing needs of its citizens.

BEGINNINGS

Very little is known about the people who originally inhabited the land that would become Liberia. When the Sahara region began to dry up, around

GRAINS OF PARADISE

The Africans in what is now Liberia first made contact with Portuguese traders because of the Europeans' need to add flavor to the dull food they stored dry for winter consumption. Aframomum melegueta *(melegueta pepper), a plant that belongs to the ginger family and is native to parts of West Africa, bore seeds that were used as a spice and a medicine. They were so highly valued that they were referred to as "grains of paradise," and in time, part of the coastal area of Liberia became known as the Grain Coast.*

2000 BCE, some of the area's residents are believed to have moved south and penetrated into West Africa. Liberia's first inhabitants were probably the descendants of these people. It is also thought that Mande-speaking tribes migrated to what would become Liberia from regions that are part of the present-day countries of Ghana and Mali. Kru tribes are thought to have been among the earliest of these arrivals, coming sometime after 1000 CE.

Beginning around 1400 CE, waves of immigration saw new tribal groups moving into modern-day Liberia from the east and north. The reasons for these population shifts are not fully known, but the conquest and decline of the ancient empire of Ghana (in present-day Mali and Mauritania) may have led some groups to flee south to escape the violence. These groups brought with them the skills of iron smelting, cloth weaving, and cotton spinning, as well as important new crops such as rice.

The identity of the first Europeans to reach Liberia has not been established, but French traders in the fourteenth and early fifteenth centuries are thought to have been the first to trade with West Africans, via trade routes that crossed the Sahara Desert from West Africa to the Mediterranean coast. In 1461, Portuguese explorers began mapping the Liberian coastline, and soon after, European traders came to collect melegueta peppers. Years later, the British and French came to the Liberian coast to collect slaves.

Early contact between Europeans and the people of the Liberian coast consisted mostly of the enslavement of the native Africans.

THE FOUNDING OF LIBERIA

In the early years of the American republic, colonization emerged as a popular response to the problem of slavery. American slaveholders were legally barred from participating in the overseas slave trade as of 1808, and Americans who sought an end to slavery looked to Africa as a solution. Colonization called for the return of slaves or free blacks to Africa, a well-meaning but flawed idea. By the early nineteenth century, most slaves had been born in the United States and had no personal connection to Africa; they would therefore be just as out of place there as they were in the American South. Moreover, no thought was given toward returning individual blacks to the specific villages or tribes from which they or their ancestors were taken—merely returning them to the continent was seen as good enough. Despite these problems, in the early nineteenth century, the Grain Coast was suggested as a possible home for freed slaves.

In 1816, the American Colonization Society (ACS) was founded, with the intention of resettling emancipated slaves and free-born African Americans. In 1818, ten years after the abolition of the slave trade, two US government officials journeyed across the Atlantic with representatives from the American Colonization Society, and together they held discussions with African tribal chiefs about acquiring enough land to form a settlement for freed slaves. When the African king Peter proved reluctant to sign over land to the society, a gun was held to his head, and his signature was obtained by force. The ACS thus acquired the area around Cape Mesurado, a small settlement that later became the capital, Monrovia. The following year, the society and six other like-minded philanthropic organizations supervised the first repatriation of freed black slaves to Africa. By 1824, the name "Liberia" had been adopted for the colony. Further settlements were founded along the coast, including the towns of Greenville and Harper, and in 1838 all of the settlements were united into the Commonwealth of Liberia. The territory expanded over the next decade, and on July 26, 1847, Governor Joseph Jenkins Roberts declared Liberia an independent state.

The coat of arms of Liberia prominently features the kind of ship that would have brought the first colonists from the United States to the African coast.

INITIAL PROBLEMS

In the early years of the settlement, the new arrivals from the United States and the Caribbean clashed with the indigenous Africans of the region. Attempts were made by local tribes to destroy the original colony at Cape Mesurado, and a clear divide emerged between the native Africans and the Americo-Liberians. The government established by the settlers was modeled after that of the United States, and it initially only held power over the towns and cities that had been established along the coast. Transport to and communication with the interior of the country, where the vast majority of the native peoples lived, was very difficult for much of the nineteenth century, and the Americo-Liberian settlers initially exercised little control over most of modern-day Liberia.

That state of affairs changed following the Berlin Conference of 1884—1885, at which the great powers of Europe divided the continent of Africa between themselves. Liberia, protected by its independent status, was not part of this division, but it was made clear that if the interior of the country was not brought under government control, it may be occupied by France or Great Britain. Motivated by this threat to the country's territorial integrity, the Americo-Liberian government moved to exert greater influence over the rain forest and mountains of Liberia's interior. This increased Liberia's population and led to more clashes between the native tribes and the Americo-Liberians. To make matters worse, the constitutional protections

The rubber trees of the Firestone plantation have been a crucial part of the Liberian economy since the 1920s.

enjoyed by the coastal cities were not extended to the country's interior, meaning the indigenous Africans—the vast majority of the population—were not guaranteed any rights or legal protections, and were instead formally subordinate to the Americo-Liberian ruling class.

Liberia also struggled with monetary woes in its first decades. The initial settlers often lacked education or any kind of training in specialized forms of labor, making it difficult for the country to develop an economy of its own. Liberia was thus heavily reliant on foreign investment and its own natural resources. The country made a healthy profit off of the export of coffee for a time, but Brazil conquered the market in the 1870s, squeezing Liberia out. Rubber was left as the country's principal export, and a plantation established by the American tire-making giant Firestone near Monrovia in 1926 quickly became the largest employer in the country and the driver of the Liberian economy for the next forty-five years.

REFORMS AND INTERNATIONAL INVOLVEMENT

In 1929, Liberia came under fire by the League of Nations (the forerunner of the United Nations) for participating in forced-labor practices that were "hardly distinguishable" from slavery. This scandal toppled the government of President Charles D. B. King, and his successor, Edwin Barclay, was compelled to end the forced-labor practices or risk Liberia becoming a mandate of the League of Nations. Forced labor was formally abolished in Liberia in 1936.

Reforms continued under the administration of President William Tubman, who was elected in 1943 and remained in office until his death in 1971. Tubman improved relations between Americo-Liberians and the indigenous population, expanding constitutional protections to include native Africans and extending the right to vote to women and indigenous property holders. Racial discrimination was outlawed in 1958, and steps were taken to better integrate the country's interior with the coastal cities. While these reforms were indeed a step in the right direction, large gulfs in income remained between the small upper class (almost exclusively Americo-Liberian) and the rest of the population (overwhelmingly indigenous Africans), which continued to live in poverty. Tubman's administration maintained the open-door economic policies of previous administrations, which welcomed foreign investment and disproportionately benefited the wealthy. Tubman was also very friendly toward Western powers, which led to a growing relationship with the United States and its allies during World War II and the Cold War that followed.

In 1942, Liberia and the United States signed a defense agreement that strengthened Liberia's previously insignificant role on the world political stage. Precipitated by the Allies' urgent wartime need of Liberia's vast rubber resources, the defense agreement resulted in the United States investing in the development of the African state's transportation infrastructure. Roads were built, and an international airport and deepwater harbor were constructed in Monrovia. Liberia was not involved in the war militarily, and it was not until January 1944 that the country officially declared war on Japan and Germany.

Liberia continued to play a broader role on the world stage after the close of World War II. It was one of the founding members of the United Nations, joining fifty other nations in ratifying the organization's original charter in 1945. Liberia then served a two-year term on the UN Security Council as a nonpermanent member beginning in 1960, and was also one of the founding member states of the Organization of African Unity (OAU) in 1963. The relationship between the United States and Liberia also continued to grow, until by the early 1970s Liberia contained the largest American embassy on the continent of Africa and served as a relay station for American diplomatic and intelligence communications.

TOLBERT AND THE MILITARY COUP

When William Tubman died in office in 1971, his vice president, William Tolbert, assumed the presidency. Tolbert was even more of a reformer than

President William Tubman began efforts to bridge the gap between the Americo-Liberians and the native population during his time in office.

his predecessor, with decided leftist sympathies. Internally, Tolbert moved to shift the Liberian economy away from Western capitalism, establishing over thirty state-owned enterprises, expanding social services, and renegotiating contracts with American and other foreign companies to make them more beneficial to the Liberian people. His foreign policy also broke with longstanding Liberian tradition. Tolbert's government recognized the Soviet Union and communist China, criticized Israel for its occupation of Palestine, and refused to grant the United States unlimited use of Liberia's main airport. Tolbert also supported Pan-African Unity, a series of movements and agreements that sought to unite the newly independent African states against lingering European colonialism.

Though the Tolbert administration took bold steps to reform Liberia and extend rights and social services to the entire population, it still faced serious challenges, and ultimately it failed to reshape Liberian society. Corruption and nepotism remained an issue under Tolbert, and despite his stated desire to expand indigenous rights and bring more native Africans into the government, his administration was still made up primarily of Americo-Liberians, who remained a distinct upper class. Tolbert's foreign policy also slowed his attempts at internal improvements, as US foreign aid to Liberia was slashed as a result of his refusal to meekly submit to American demands. A fall in world prices for rubber and iron ore plunged the country into an economic slump, and the Central Intelligence Agency (CIA) began actively supporting groups that formed in opposition to the president.

When the government placed a higher import tax on rice in 1980 to stimulate domestic production, anti-government demonstrations took place. Opposition leaders and organizations believed that Tolbert was trying to increase profits for rice importers and make more money for his own family, which was one of the largest producers of rice in the country. The American government supported these protesters, some of whom were eventually imprisoned when they called for a general strike. Finally, on April 12, 1980, a military coup led by Master Sergeant Samuel K. Doe was carried out, which resulted in the murder of William Tolbert in the middle of the night. According to eyewitnesses, Doe received the blessing and backing of the US embassy on the night of the coup.

After taking control of the state at the head of his People's Redemption Council, Doe quickly moved to consolidate his power and reverse most of Tolbert's attempts at reform. Thirteen of Tolbert's cabinet ministers and aides were publicly executed on a beach while news cameras broadcast the bloody footage to the world, the constitution was suspended, and hundreds of dissidents were imprisoned or executed. Doe also cut ties with governments that were hostile to the United States and the West and granted the American military unlimited access to the country and its airfields. This renewed friendliness to American economic and military interests was met with reciprocal friendliness on the part of the United States, which increased the amount of foreign aid granted to Liberia from $20 million in 1979 to more than $120 million in 1982. During his nine years in power, Doe received more than half a billion dollars from the United States.

President William Tolbert made serious efforts toward political and economic reform, but was assassinated in a military coup in 1980.

The cordial relationship did not last, however. Under pressure from the United States and other Western nations to at least put up a façade of democracy, Doe called for elections in 1985. These elections were the first in Liberia's history that featured multiple political parties and in which millions of people, both indigenous and Americo-Liberian, participated. Unfortunately, Doe rigged the result, and though one of his rivals almost certainly won the popular vote, Doe declared himself president and was formally sworn in in 1986. Between this power grab and a growing resistance to listening to advisors, both foreign and domestic, Doe's rule became increasingly erratic and unstable, crumbling the relationship between Doe's government and the United States. With strong American support no longer in place, Doe's rule became vulnerable to the many armed groups that formed in opposition to his dictatorship.

THE LIBERIAN CIVIL WAR AND ITS AFTERMATH

On December 24, 1989, a rebel army led by Charles Taylor crossed into Liberia from the Ivory Coast. Calling itself the National Patriotic Front of

Samuel Doe, in dark sunglasses, addresses the Liberian people shortly after his coup in April 1980.

Liberia (NPFL), Taylor's army began a civil war that would last for the better part of the next fourteen years. Numerous other armed factions sprang up during the civil war, many of which were formed along ethnic lines.

The initial conflict pitted the Krahn and Mandingo supporters of Doe against the Gio and Mano forces of Taylor, but over the course of the civil war, alliances shifted and more tribes entered the fray. One group that split from the NPFL in the early days of the war, led by Prince Johnson, captured, tortured, and killed Samuel Doe in 1990. Both Johnson and Taylor claimed in later years that they had received funding, training, and support from the United States and its allies.

A fragile peace was briefly achieved in 1997, after seven and a half years of war. Taylor had declared himself president and established a capital in Gbarnga following Prince Johnson's seizure of Monrovia and execution of Doe, and fighting between these forces (as well as the many other ethnic factions involved in the conflict) dragged on through several attempts at making peace. Finally, with the signing of the Abuja Accord in 1996, tens of thousands of fighters agreed to lay down their arms, and an election was scheduled for 1997. Charles Taylor had emerged from the civil war in the best position to take power, and the election, judged fair by outside observers, saw him win over 75 percent of the vote; the Liberian people were anxious to avoid further war and thought that allowing Taylor to formally take power would be the easiest way to achieve peace.

Peace was not to be had, however. Taylor's government proved to be brutal and oppressive, targeting dissidents and human rights activists. Liberia's infrastructure had also been devastated by the civil war, and foreign investors were hesitant to put money into a country just emerging from heavy fighting. Charles Taylor himself failed to inspire confidence in the stability of Liberia, particularly after he was accused of abetting war crimes in the neighboring country of Sierra Leone. By 1999, the civil war had resumed, with multiple

THE 1980 COUP

Only four members of William Tolbert's government were not executed by Samuel Doe after the military coup. One of them was Tolbert's minister of finance, Ellen Johnson Sirleaf, who would later go on to be elected president of Liberia in 2005.

small armies working to topple Taylor's government. Accusations that Taylor had sold weapons to rebels in Sierra Leone in exchange for blood diamonds prompted the United Nations to enforce an arms embargo on Liberia in 2001, and in June 2003, Taylor was indicted for war crimes by a UN tribunal.

The indictment came during peace talks to end the civil war, and it did little to help Taylor's bargaining position. He said he was willing to leave the country if it would lead to peace, and troops from the United States, the United Nations, and other African states arrived in Liberia in August 2003 to force Taylor to abide by his word. Taylor fled to Nigeria, and a peace accord was signed by the interim government and the rebels soon after. With the war finally over, American soldiers left Liberia, though a UN mission of fifteen thousand troops remained in the country to ensure the peace deal remained in place and to protect the Liberian people. This mission stayed in the country until 2016, when responsibility for internal security was formally turned over to the Liberian army and police.

In all, Liberia's civil war resulted in the deaths of between 150,000 and 250,000 people, and displaced almost 1 million more. Around 250,000 Liberians became refugees as a result of the war; of these, more than 150,000 were helped to repatriate to Liberia by the UN Refugee Agency, while many others returned to the country on their own.

THE JOHNSON SIRLEAF ADMINISTRATION

Following the devastation wrought by fourteen years of civil war, Liberia faced massive challenges in restoring stable political institutions, rebuilding the country's economy, and taking care of its war-weary populace. Elections were held to form a new government in 2005, and many parties participated.

Charles Taylor, as the leader of the NPFL, was the most prominent political figure during the Liberian civil war.

The elections were free and fair, and the winner was Ellen Johnson Sirleaf, who became the first female elected head of state in the history of the African continent, taking office in January 2006. An indigenous Liberian by ancestry, Johnson Sirleaf had served in William Tolbert's government in the 1970s before spending most of the next two decades outside of Liberia. Though she faced a daunting task in taking power over a country that had been nearly destroyed by civil war, her first term in office saw her make real progress toward bringing Liberia out from the shadow of violence.

Promising to fight corruption and restore foreign investment in the country, Johnson Sirleaf took advantage of her contacts in the United States and elsewhere, forged during her years in exile, to bring humanitarian aid and business investment back to Liberia. Unlike Charles Taylor, whose propensity for violence and oppression discouraged outside investment in Liberia, Johnson Sirleaf successfully restored the open-door economic policy of William Tubman and his predecessors. The Liberian economy grew as a result, and the money coming into the country also allowed Johnson Sirleaf to make improvements to the health-care system and start rebuilding the infrastructure damaged or destroyed during the civil war. Power was partially restored to Monrovia for the first time in fifteen years, and the UN lifted its embargoes on arms sales and timber and diamond exports. In 2010, Johnson Sirleaf's government came to an agreement with the International Monetary Fund (IMF) and the World Bank to pardon $1.2 billion in debt, removing a massive financial burden from the government. In 2011, Ellen Johnson Sirleaf was a corecipient of the Nobel Peace Prize for her efforts to secure peace, promote economic and social development, and strengthen the position of women.

The Johnson Sirleaf administration did not escape criticism, however. Despite her promise to fight corruption, millions of dollars in humanitarian donations went unaccounted for, and some legislators were bribed to approve offshore oil concessions or other business deals. Though these incidents were brought to the attention of Johnson Sirleaf, her administration did little to actually combat this corruption. She also continued the longstanding practice of appointing family members to government positions—three of her sons and a nephew were given official jobs within her administration. More broadly, for the majority of Liberians, the economic gains made during the Johnson Sirleaf administration had no impact on their lives; most remained as poor as they were during the civil war.

Johnson Sirleaf herself was also criticized, not only for the areas in which her administration was lacking but for statements she made to the Truth and Reconciliation Commission, which she had organized in the early days of her presidency to impartially examine the causes and conduct of the civil war and to offer guidance for how the country could best move forward. Johnson Sirleaf admitted to the commission that she had supported Charles Taylor and the NPFL during the first days of the civil war, but she downplayed the intensity and duration of her involvement. Nevertheless, Johnson Sirleaf was included in the commission's list of Liberians who should be barred from holding public office as a consequence for their participation in the civil war. When Johnson Sirleaf ran for reelection in 2011, the commission's finding was used against her by her opponents, as was the timing of the announcement that she had been awarded the Nobel Prize. Coming just weeks before the election, Johnson Sirleaf's opponents questioned whether the award had been meant to influence the vote, especially since it directly contradicted the censure Johnson Sirleaf had received from the Truth and Reconciliation Commission.

Though Johnson Sirleaf did win the election, it was not without controversy, as her opponent in the second round of balloting boycotted the vote, citing the Nobel Prize as well as voting irregularities in the first round as reasons that the election should be considered illegitimate. Johnson Sirleaf was nonetheless sworn in for her second term in 2012, and in June 2016, she was elected to head the Economic Community of West African States (ECOWAS), an economic union comprising fifteen countries.

Ellen Johnson Sirleaf *(far right)* was the first elected female president in Africa and corecipient of the 2011 Nobel Peace Prize.

"The hardest part of the war was people starving—everyone was malnourished and that was truly terrible to see." —Pandora Hodge

THE EBOLA CRISIS

This health-care worker disinfects areas around a hospital. The Ebola virus virtually shut down the country of Liberia for an extended period of time in 2014 and 2015.

In 2014, Liberia was struck with a new disaster, in the form of an Ebola virus epidemic that raged across several West African nations. Transmitted through the bodily fluids of an infected person (or corpse), the Ebola virus causes severe fever, vomiting, muscle weakness, and, if left untreated, uncontrollable bleeding, organ failure, and death. Beginning in rural villages in early 2014, the virus spread to the city of Monrovia in May, at which time infection rates soared. Those who caught the disease usually passed it on to several other people, creating an exponential progression of infection that eventually overwhelmed the Liberian health-care system. By August, treatment centers were full, and there were bodies lying in the streets of Monrovia. About three thousand American military personnel were sent to West Africa to help build health facilities and train health-care workers, and the Centers for Disease Control and Prevention (CDC) and Doctors Without Borders (MSF) took the lead in treating patients. As the crisis deepened, schools and markets were closed to prevent large public gatherings, air traffic was grounded, and international businesses closed their doors indefinitely. By the time Liberia was declared Ebola-free in June 2016, more than 4,800 people had died; in all of West Africa, the death toll reached 11,300.

Though the Ebola crisis affected several nations in the region, Liberia fared worse than its neighbors. Traditional cultural practices and distrust of the government combined with the country's poor infrastructure to produce this result. Ancestral medicinal and burial practices, originating from both Islam and tribal religious beliefs, played a major role in prolonging the crisis. Many Liberians insisted on treating their infected loved ones at home, which only served to spread the disease to the rest of the family. Traditional burial customs, which require the family to wash and bury the bodies of their loved ones themselves, also expanded the rates of infection. These ritual practices in some cases led to the deaths of entire families in the countryside.

Even outside of the rural villages, however, many Liberians fell victim to the Ebola virus because of their distrust of the government, cultivated during the civil war and the decade that followed. When these citizens heard the government warning of Ebola, they reacted with doubt and skepticism, cynically dismissing it as a scheme to generate more foreign aid. The presence of foreign doctors and troops in the country was also seen to be an attempt by the United States to exert more influence over Liberia and nothing more. Only after local leaders and tribal healers—people whom the average Liberian trusted— began urging residents to take precautions against the virus did the disease finally begin to abate.

Liberia is still dealing with the lingering effects of the Ebola epidemic, which include an economic slowdown and an uptick in other diseases, caused when the ban on public gatherings during the height of the crisis prevented mass immunization campaigns from being carried out. It is these challenges, together with the ongoing projects to rebuild the country's infrastructure and expand basic services to the majority of the population, that will define Liberia in the years to come.

INTERNET LINKS

https://www.theatlantic.com/magazine/archive/2016/07/after-ebola/485609
This article details the aftermath of the Ebola virus in Liberia.

http://www.bbc.com/news/world-africa-13732188
This BBC timeline spotlights major events in Liberian history.

https://www.britannica.com/place/Liberia
The Encyclopedia Britannica article on Liberia contains information about not just the history of the country but also about its government, economy, and people. A subscription is required to view the full article.

GOVERNMENT

The modern-day Executive Mansion is located in Monrovia, Liberia.

3

THE GOVERNMENT OF LIBERIA HAS only recently reasserted its power after years of military dictatorship and civil war. In 2005, democratic elections brought Ellen Johnson Sirleaf to power, and her administration sought to restore political stability and governmental accountability to a country that had experienced neither for generations.

Liberia's earliest constitution followed the example of the United States. Like the original US Constitution, in Liberia's constitution, many parts of the country's population were not treated as equals. As a result, a political elite developed among the early Americo-Liberians and their descendants. Under the presidency of William Tubman (1943–1971), some attempts were made to deal with this problem by extending the vote to all adults, including women, who paid taxes and owned property. This was not universal suffrage, however, and it made little difference to most Liberians.

President William Tolbert's administration (1971–1980) did bring about genuine reform. Universal suffrage was introduced for all Liberians over the age of eighteen, and the constitution was amended so that no president could stand for reelection. Regrettably, Tolbert's reforms were short lived, as the military coup launched by Samuel Doe resulted in the suspension of the constitution and the suppression of most Liberians' rights. A new constitution, drafted and adopted in 1984, was largely the same as the document it had been designed to replace.

"And now, this year, 2017, (Liberia) will witness an historic transfer of power, providing the basis for consolidation of post-conflict democracy; where the future will be transferred to the next generation of Liberians."
—President Ellen Johnson Sirleaf

The Liberian
Supreme Court
is housed in the
Temple of Justice,
often the site
of protests, as
pictured here.

pattern developed among some of the tribes in the northwest part of the country. This region had a relatively unstable past, and opportunities arose for individuals to emerge as leaders through force and acquired wealth, rather than by accident of birth.

One of the duties of tribal chiefs is to mediate disputes between villagers, including those caused by the breakup of a marriage. In these instances, the families involved are often eager to divide the couple's goods to their own advantage. The husband's family seeks to reacquire their dowry, or bride price, while the wife aims to keep it as compensation for her years of work. It is the chief's job to forge an agreement that will be acceptable to all parties involved, since they must all live together as neighbors after the divorce is complete.

CRIMINAL JUSTICE

A system of criminal law based on Western systems of justice has always existed in Liberia. This includes courts of law, judges, and trials by jury. The Liberian Supreme Court is made up of a chief justice and four associate justices, all of whom are appointed by the president. Unfortunately, the Western system of law has historically only functioned effectively in the area around the capital and in large towns and cities. Even there, however, politicians have been known to manipulate the law to their political and personal advantage. These corrupt tendencies were exacerbated by the military dictatorship and the ensuing civil war, which saw the criminal justice system collapse entirely, replaced with summary justice at the hands of individual warring factions.

Rural areas have often existed beyond the reach of the criminal justice system and have seen more traditional methods of tribal justice employed by chiefs and village elders. These traditional tribal laws depend for their success on the respect that is accorded to the local chiefs, and there are no written guidelines to ensure their consistent application. One traditional form of justice that is still occasionally practiced in Liberia is trial by ordeal. In this custom, a person accused of a serious crime is made to endure a painful ritual as a test of integrity and honesty—for example, drinking a poison made from the bark of the sasswood tree. The thinking behind this practice supposes that a guilty person will find it difficult to maintain the bluff of innocence when faced with the possibility of death by poison, and will therefore confess to their crime. Though trial by ordeal is now illegal in Liberia, it is still practiced by some rural tribes behind the backs of (or with tacit permission from) government officials.

While the administration of President Johnson Sirleaf took massive strides in restoring law and order to Liberia, much work remains to be done.

Liberian police officers assumed full responsibility for keeping the peace in Liberia after the last United Nations troops left the country in the summer of 2016.

Liberians went to the polls on October 10, 2017, to elect a new president. That election resulted in two final candidates: George Weah and Joseph Boakai. However, another round of voting was needed to determine the final outcome. The date agreed upon was November 7, 2017. However, the day before that election, Liberia's Supreme Court announced the election would be delayed. The reason was that Charles

Brumskine, the third-place finisher in the October 10 election, had expressed concern over the first election results, suggesting the possibility of fraud. An investigation was conducted, and it was resolved by December. The runoff election finally took place on December 26, 2017. George Weah was chosen as the next president of Liberia.

Prior to the October election, sitting president Ellen Johnson Sirleaf was not constitutionally permitted to run again, so she threw her support behind her vice president, Joseph Boakai. Nineteen other candidates also ran for the presidency, including George Weah, known as a soccer star and a 2005 presidential candidate, and Prince Johnson, the senior senator from Nimba County and former warlord who executed Samuel Doe during the civil war. Liberia had around two million registered voters before the intended election, and efforts were carried out to register hundreds of thousands more in anticipation of the October date. Of particular interest to registration activists was bringing more women into the political process. Women are 26 percent less likely than men to be registered to vote in Liberia, and 43 percent fewer women than men voted in the 2014 Senate elections.

Though President Johnson Sirleaf was the first elected female head of state in Africa's history, the rest of the government is still overwhelmingly male (women make up only 10 percent of the National Assembly). Activists hope that encouraging more women to participate in the political process will not only lead to more women eventually running for and achieving office, but will also force male representatives to take their female constituents into account when considering legislation.

The Liberian police regularly steal from the citizenry, make arbitrary arrests designed to "send a message" rather than protect the public, and occasionally beat detainees severely, in some cases resulting in the victim's death. Reports have also been made of sexual exploitation by both the police and the UN peacekeepers. Liberian prisons are understaffed and underfunded, in some cases having no clean water, health care, or even regular meals for the inmates. There is also a major problem with overcrowding. Some prisons mix juveniles with adults, and at one point in 2016, Monrovia Central Prison was found to contain almost 1,000 prisoners—more than two-and-a-half times its capacity of 375 inmates. The judicial system is vulnerable to bribery, of both judges and prosecutors, and defendants, though legally entitled to a defense attorney, are often denied this right if they cannot afford to pay for it. These problems are not unique to Liberia, of course, and can be found to greater or lesser degrees in even the most developed Western nations, but they do show the need for continued criminal justice reform in Liberia in the years ahead.

INTERNET LINKS

http://emansion.gov.lr
The official website for Liberia's Executive Mansion includes information about the president and vice president, transcripts of official speeches, and links to other ministries within the Liberian government.

http://www.lr.undp.org/content/liberia/en/home/presscenter/ articles/2017/04/12/more-than-two-million-liberians-register-to- vote-almost-half-are-women
This article focuses on the efforts of the United Nations Development Program (UNDP) and Liberian organizations to register new voters in time for the October 2017 presidential election.

ECONOMY

Agricultural work is the most common form of labor in Liberia. Here, women work a vegetable field in Kakata.

O VER THE PAST FEW DECADES, THE Liberian economy has suffered multiple system shocks, including the military coup in 1980, the civil war in the 1990s, and the Ebola crisis in 2014. As a result, it has struggled to grow with any consistency, leaving Liberia an incredibly poor country.

Approximately 84 percent of Liberians are forced to survive on less than 1.25 US dollars per day; 60 percent of the country does not even earn a dollar. The Liberian population is also incredibly young— 60 percent of Liberians are below the age of twenty-five, including 42 percent who are fourteen years old or younger. This exacerbates the problem of poverty, as most workers are attempting to support multiple children on extremely little money. It also means that the crisis posed by low wages is bound to get worse, as children and young adults will all need employment sooner rather than later.

The largest field of employment in Liberia is agriculture, with seven out of ten Liberian workers earning their living on the land. Despite this, agriculture only accounts for 44 percent of Liberia's gross domestic product (GDP), meaning the vast majority of farmers are earning little reward for their labor. In a further example of the economic disparity in the country, more women than men are engaged in agriculture, despite men accounting for 60 percent of the labor force. Another consequence of Liberia's dependence on agriculture for employment is that consumer goods, raw materials, and even foodstuffs have to be imported on a mass

4

"(African nations) must diversify (their) economies and invest in small transformative industries." —President Ellen Johnson Sirleaf

scale, mainly from the Far East. This has produced a massive trade deficit, as the cost of the goods being brought into the country is more than five times the value of those that are sold abroad.

Areas of employment outside of agriculture include manufacturing and various types of administration and service jobs. While these jobs occasionally pay better than agricultural work and may even include basic labor protections and benefits, they are also out of reach for the majority of the population, who lack the education to qualify for them.

ECONOMIC TURMOIL

The political instability experienced by Liberia since the 1980s has led to an equal degree of economic uncertainty. The economy was devastated by the fourteen-year-long civil war that brought the country to a standstill, and just when it looked like peace had been restored and the economy was on a path toward steady growth, it was ground to a halt once again by the Ebola crisis. With the disease outbreak now over, Liberia is at the start of a now-familiar process of economic reconstruction.

The civil war did incredible damage to Liberia's economy, and its long-term effects are still being felt. The constant fighting damaged the country's infrastructure, including its roads, bridges, and ports, as well as much of its industry. The war also left more than three-quarters of Liberians unemployed. Its consequences even extended beyond the country's borders, as foreign investment, historically a crucial part of Liberia's economy, dried up. Businesspeople, like many other citizens, fled the country, taking with them their skills and capital, and the tourism industry, though never a major economic asset, was nevertheless wiped out.

Perhaps the most damaging consequence of the war was its effect on the country's education system. The war caused the closure of many schools and the collapse of the vocational programs that had been initiated by the government in the years before the civil war. As a result, a generation of Liberians grew up with almost no education and was therefore unqualified for most skilled labor. This had a negative impact not only on the personal and familial financial stability of the particular Liberians affected, but also on the economy as a whole, as these individuals were largely unable to work in any field besides agriculture.

Under President Johnson Sirleaf, the Liberian economy began to improve. With the war over, Johnson Sirleaf was able to bring foreign investment back into the country and begin work on repairing its damaged infrastructure. This led to steady economic growth from year to year, and a rise in the per capita GDP. While the vast majority of the economic gains went to a small circle of wealthy Liberians and the lives of most citizens were identical in 2013 to what they had been in 2003, the economic stability had at the very least prevented things from getting any worse.

Liberian currency has struggled to appreciate in value since the end of the civil war.

With the Ebola crisis, that stability was shattered. Businesses were closed, foreign investment froze, and the government was forced to redirect money that had been intended for infrastructure improvements to health care. Economic growth fell to a statistical zero from 2014 to 2016, at the same time that commodity prices decreased worldwide, leading to inflation within Liberia. Though the disease has been successfully combatted, the government still faces challenges in putting the economy back on track. The crisis reduced the amount of revenue generated by the government, forcing it to decrease its budget and hampering its ability to make renewed investments in internal improvements. The government is also newly responsible for fully funding the country's security forces, as the peacekeepers stationed in the country by the United Nations departed the country in 2016. Still, the economy is expected to grow 2 to 5 percent over the next few years, as a result of increased gold production, mining activity, and agricultural productivity.

NATURAL RESOURCES

Liberia's most important natural resources are rubber and iron ore, though timber, diamonds, gold, and various metals and minerals are also found in the country.

Latex is collected in a cup to produce rubber, Liberia's most important natural resource.

In 1926, the American company Firestone acquired the first rubber plantation in Liberia, and it quickly began exporting rubber around the world. At one point, Liberia was the largest rubber producer in all of Africa, and Firestone employed around ten thousand people at its plantations. Though Liberia's rubber production is no longer a world leader, rubber is still an important driver of the country's economy, accounting for more than 75 percent of total exports in the years following the 2003 peace accord. Firestone remains a major employer in Liberia today, though it has become a subject of controversy for its labor practices.

Liberia's tropical rain forest, a source of hardwood timber, was an important part of President Johnson Sirleaf's plan for economic revival. The government operates a system of concessions that gives companies—often foreign-owned—the right to harvest a predetermined area of forest in return for a fee. This program greatly helped boost the country's economy in the years following the end of the civil war, prompting Johnson Sirleaf to

IRON ORE

In the 1960s, the production of rubber— until then Liberia's most important industry—was for the first time outstripped by the mining of iron ore. Large deposits of iron ore were discovered in the 1940s in the mountainous terrain in the north of the country, and within two decades iron ore had become the country's principal export.

Iron ore exports remain an important part of the Liberian economy today, and thousands of Liberians are employed by mining companies.

OIL

One of the hopes of the Johnson Sirleaf administration during its economic recovery efforts was that Liberia would be able to find oil off of the Atlantic coast. Though offshore deposits thought to contain potentially one billion barrels of oil were believed to exist for many years, the efforts to access these deposits have been unsuccessful. ExxonMobil and other oil giants have so far drilled ten wells off the coast of Liberia and have yet to find any deposits of commercial quantity. Some experts point to a similar situation that took place when the nearby country of Ghana was developing its oil industry, in which it took fifty drilled wells to finally find one of sufficient size, as a reason for Liberia to continue pursuing its exploration efforts. In the meantime, however, the country will continue to be reliant on imported oil.

overreach in 2012 and license companies to cut down 58 percent of the rain forest in the country. This proposal was met with heavy international criticism from environmentalists and conservationists, as well as internal criticism from Liberians who feared that the concessions would only benefit wealthy foreign industrialists at the expense of ordinary citizens. Johnson Sirleaf revoked many of the permits in response, and in 2014, her administration signed a deal with the Norwegian government to reform forest governance. Part of that deal involved a freeze on new logging concessions, effectively capping the amount of timber that can be harvested in the country.

Conversely, the Liberian government has recently succeeded in expanding its use of water as a source of energy. The Mount Coffee hydropower plant on the Saint Paul River was finally rehabilitated and reopened in 2016, and it is expected that the plant will expand access to electricity to hundreds of thousands of Liberians.

THE COCONUT PALM

A vital component of the village economy is the coconut palm tree, which is used limb, leaf, and nut by Liberians. Its branches are used in building houses and thatching, while the leaves are stripped and turned into string and raffia, from which villagers make baskets, nets, and even clothes. The fruit is used to make cooking oil, candles, soap, cosmetics, and palm wine. The inner nuts are dried to make nut meat that can be stored or sold, and the shells are burned to make ash for soap. Even the trunk is used to make kitchen utensils, brooms, and fences.

AGRICULTURE

The principal area of employment in the country, most farms in Liberia are small and belong to a single family. A typical small farmer grows rice, cassava, and vegetables, and raises such animals as goats, chickens, sheep, and ducks. These animals have cash value and provide an important source of food for the family's own needs. Farmers also earn cash by cultivating coffee, cacao, oil palms, swamp rice, and sugarcane. Many farmers are members of local cooperatives, which pay individual farmers for their cash crops and in turn sell the bulk crops to larger merchants.

The cultivation of rice makes an essential contribution to the feeding of the country's population, but because the yield is low, a significant quantity of rice also needs to be imported every year. The country's poor infrastructure also makes imports of foodstuffs necessary. To take one example, the poor condition of Liberia's roads makes it cheaper to import rice to Monrovia

from Thailand, 7,500 miles (12,070 km) away, than to bring the rice overland from Gbarnga, the agricultural community that lies only 100 miles (161 km) outside of the capital city.

Rural Liberians harvest rice, a principal source of food in the country.

TRANSPORTATION PROBLEMS

More than a decade after the civil war came to a close, Liberia's transportation network still faces serious challenges. The country has over 6,600 miles (10,600 km) of roads, but a small percentage are paved. The rest are dirt tracks, nearly three-quarters of which are not passable year round.

The lack of well-made, passable roads has had a remarkable impact on the country. When dirt roads wash out during the rainy season, rural areas become virtually inaccessible, preventing residents from bringing their goods to the markets or sending their children to school, and delaying the arrival of food or medical care. The crumbling transportation network is therefore slowing economic progress, hampering improvements in health-care outcomes and education, and contributing to the struggles faced by so many Liberians in their daily lives. The Johnson Sirleaf administration, together with international organizations, including the World Bank, invested in road repair and construction in an effort to solve these problems. One such project rehabilitated the Suakoko Highway, a 153-mile (246 km) stretch of road that connects Monrovia with Gbarnga and the Guinea border. The improved road has not only eased vehicular traffic and made it easier for farmers to get their goods to market, but it has also spurred the development of towns and

Dirt roads make up the majority of Liberia's transportation system.

cities along the road. As they are now seeing more visitors, these cities have invested in the construction of hotels and shopping centers. The project also provides for the maintenance of these roads, a task that has created 1,400 jobs.

Liberia's railroad network was also devastated by the civil war. At one time consisting of three major lines and 267 miles (430 km) of track built to transport iron ore to the port of Monrovia, the railways were left inoperable by the conflict. Bits of the rails were sold for scrap by cash-strapped Liberians. As of 2017, efforts to revive the rail systems have been made, and more than half of Liberia's original rail capacity has been restored.

The country has a total of twenty-nine airports, but only two contain paved runways. The others consist mainly of small airfields in the interior of the country. The international airport, built by the United States during World War II, is situated to the east of the capital.

Roberts International Airport is Liberia's primary airport.

INTERNET LINKS

https://www.afdb.org/en/countries/west-africa/liberia/liberia-economic-outlook
The African Development Bank Group outlines the challenges facing Liberia's economy and provides projections for the country's economic future.

http://www.worldbank.org/en/country/liberia/overview
The World Bank's overview of its projects in Liberia contains not only a summary of the nation's economic outlook but also a report on the results of the organization's work in the country.

ENVIRONMENT

Liberia faces a number of challenges in preserving its rain forests.

5

L IKE SO MANY ASPECTS OF LIFE IN Liberia, the environment was neglected amid the strife and destruction of two decades of civil war and political upheaval.

Liberia's rich natural resources—especially diamonds and timber—were, in part, a source of conflict, as the warring factions sought to control the products that would finance their military operations. Now that peace has returned to Liberia, environmental issues have become more important than ever. Under President Ellen Johnson Sirleaf, the Liberian government made addressing environmental concerns a top priority, investing in programs to combat climate change, tackle deforestation, improve sanitation services, and collect refuse.

These are not merely issues of concern to environmentalists. Rather, they are part of a broader strategy by the government to improve the lives of all Liberians. The nation's low life expectancy (fifty-nine years) is in part a consequence of unsanitary living conditions, lack of clean drinking water, and poor air quality in the cities. The lives, health, and material prosperity of Liberians will not improve until good sanitation and safe drinking water are available to all. This makes addressing Liberia's environmental needs an issue of paramount importance.

CLIMATE CHANGE

Of the many environmental challenges facing Liberia, none is more threatening in the long term than that posed by climate change. Temperatures in Liberia increased by 1.44°F (0.8°C) between 1960 and 2006, and are expected to continue increasing at a steadily growing rate for the rest of the twenty-first century. The heavy deforestation carried out in Liberia has contributed to these rising temperatures, as fewer

"With 43 percent of the biodiversity in the West African region, Liberia is mindful of the imperative of protecting the environment from the trappings of global warming and the effects of climate change."
—President Ellen Johnson Sirleaf

trees exist to absorb carbon dioxide from the atmosphere. At the same time that temperatures are going up, the average annual rainfall received by the country has actually dropped since 1960, though increased downpours and flooding events during the rainy season have been recorded. These heavy rainfall events are expected to increase in frequency going forward, together with a rise in sea levels of 2 to 3.3 feet (0.6—1 m).

The effects of climate change could prove disastrous for Liberia. The potential increases in flooding threaten agricultural production and livestock grazing, which would in turn result in reduced food supplies and increased prices. Warming ocean temperatures also threaten fish stocks, another important source of food. The erosion caused by rising sea levels would pose a major challenge for the country, as 58 percent of the population lives along the coast, together with much of the country's agricultural and energy production centers. Increased precipitation during the rainy season threatens to overwhelm the wetlands and other natural flood barriers native to the region, and can also pollute the country's water supply, increasing the risk of cholera and other waterborne diseases. The effects of climate change will disproportionately impact the poor, who will suffer most keenly from food shortages and disease outbreaks. If the effects of, and crises caused by, climate change are severe enough, they could even risk shattering the country's fragile peace and plunging it back into conflict.

In response, the Johnson Sirleaf administration partnered with international aid agencies to develop renewable energy strategies and adapt the country to the changing climate conditions. The Environmental Protection Agency (EPA) was created in 2003, and in 2008 the National Adaptation Programme of Action (NAPA) was drafted to help put the country on a path to green energy and climate stability. Unfortunately, the steps taken toward addressing climate change have been halted by institutional barriers. The exact roles of the country's regulatory agencies are not clear, and there has been a frustrating lack of cooperation among them. The government is also unable to fully fund these agencies, limiting the amount of oversight and monitoring that can be carried out. Despite these problems, Liberia has made progress in protecting its environment, and the country is taking the challenge posed by climate change very seriously.

DEFORESTATION

Another challenge inextricably linked to climate change is the damage done by rampant deforestation. Trees are cut down in mass quantities in Liberia to either sell as timber or to clear land for farming, and the process has wreaked havoc on the environment. Liberia's forests make up 44.5 percent of the remaining unspoiled rain forests in all of West Africa and are home to thousands of species of plants and animals,

Massive areas of forest are cleared every year in Liberia, the trees stripped and sold as timber.

many of which are virtually extinct elsewhere in the region. The loss of habitat has led to declining numbers for many of these populations, throwing entire ecosystems into chaos. Deforestation also contributes heavily to climate change, as it results in fewer trees being available to absorb carbon dioxide from the atmosphere. Finally, the forest provides shelter for the cultural and religious practices of the people who live nearby, who are deeply impacted by the harvesting of timber.

Industrial-scale deforestation began in the 1970s, when large areas of jungle were cleared for the development of coffee, rubber, and oil palm plantations. Logging continued throughout the 1980s and exploded during the civil war in the 1990s, when there was no governmental oversight whatsoever. Massive logging concessions were then granted to timber companies in the late 1990s by Charles Taylor, who was hoping to use the money to reconstruct the country and achieve stability. Though he failed in this goal, the basic idea remained attractive to his successor, Ellen Johnson Sirleaf. She also granted massive concessions to foreign logging companies, culminating in the consigning of 58 percent of the country's forest resources to destruction in 2012. At a time when over 74,000 acres (30,000 hectares) of forest were already being cleared on a yearly basis, half of which was being logged illegally, this move provoked intense criticism from both the Liberian people and the international community.

Under pressure, Johnson Sirleaf revoked some of the permits, and in 2014, her administration signed a $150 million deal with the Norwegian government to help move Liberia toward a deforestation-free future. The deal provides money for Liberia to invest in policing illegal logging with the long-term goal of bringing deforestation to a halt in the country, thereby reducing greenhouse gas emissions. No new logging concessions will be granted until the existing licenses are reviewed by an independent body, and 30 percent of Liberia's forests are to be placed under protected status by 2020. Though still in its early years, the deal has proven successful so far—large companies have stopped logging while their licenses are being reviewed, and companies seeking new concessions are being forced to meet sustainability requirements, planting new trees to replace those they plan on harvesting.

A small visitors' hut marks the entrance to Sapo National Park.

Liberia's forests are believed to contain more than two thousand varieties of flowering plants, hundreds of which have medicinal value.

FOREST RESERVES

Until 2003, only one-quarter of the forest in Liberia's Sapo National Park (which has a total area of 698 square miles/1,808 sq km) was classified as protected land. This allowed loggers, farmers, and plantations to exploit the majority of the forest without restriction. In 2002, conservationists sought to educate people about the damage being done to the forest and its native wildlife by setting up a soccer league with players drawn from villages around the park. Teams were named after local animals to encourage people to protect and be proud of the environment. Shortly after, the government moved to designate all of Sapo National Park as a protected area.

Liberia has also created the East Nimba Nature Reserve, adding protected forest within its borders to the larger Nimba Nature Reserve, which stretches across the borders of Guinea and the Ivory Coast. The Grebo Forest Reserve in

Since 1997, Fauna and Flora International has made Liberia the central pillar of its West African conservation program. In 2001, it became the first international environmental group to establish an office in Liberia, and since then it has been responsible for several major environmental improvements. The group helped expand Sapo National Park, one of the least disturbed forest ecosystems in West Africa, and was instrumental in creating the East Nimba Nature Reserve. The organization has also taken a leading role in fighting deforestation. In 2013, a new conservation center was opened at Sapo National Park, initiated and operated by Fauna and Flora International. The center will help train forestry professionals in Liberia and allow ecological and socioeconomic research to take place.

the east of the country is home to an amazing array of wildlife, including the pygmy hippopotamus and chimpanzee. The conservation organization Fauna and Flora International has established a program to protect the chimpanzee, which has seen its numbers decrease by 75 percent in the last thirty years as a result of poaching, trafficking, and habitat loss. Other international

The chimpanzee is one of several endangered animals living in the rain forests of Liberia.

The common kusimanse is a relative of the mongoose and is native to the jungles of West Africa.

conservation organizations have been invited to Liberia to assess the condition of the nation's biodiversity.

ENDANGERED SPECIES

The damage to and loss of rain forest has had a serious impact on wildlife in Liberia. The animal population is in rapid decline, and some species, including the pygmy hippopotamus, the elephant, and the leopard, are almost extinct. In the less densely forested coastal areas, hunting and the conversion of forest to farmland have decimated wildlife, and there are no longer any large herds of big game in the interior of the country. The poaching of wild animals for food has also increased, especially since the roads created by logging operations have allowed hunters greater access to the forests than ever before.

Many species in Liberia are endangered or vulnerable to becoming endangered, and these animals will only continue to decrease in number as their habitats are destroyed. Among the most endangered are the pygmy hippopotamus, the Jentink's duiker, and the chimpanzee. Other vulnerable species include the African elephant, the Liberian mongoose, and the African manatee.

SANITATION

A major obstacle to both environmental improvements and public health is Liberia's crumbling or nonexistent sanitation infrastructure. The vast majority of the country lacks access to clean water or sanitation facilities, leading to ill health, diminished education outcomes, and a loss of economic productivity.

Only 25 percent of Liberians have regular access to clean water, and half have no access to toilets. Though the destruction of water treatment facilities during the civil war was a major cause of this sanitation emergency, things have improved very little in the years since the war ended. The problem is also not relegated to rural areas; poor city planning, congested housing, and no requirements that landlords provide toilets have led to a sanitation crisis in the heart of the capital. At one point in the late 2000s, the seventy thousand residents of the West Point slum in Monrovia were forced to share thirty-two public restrooms with a total of four functioning toilets.

While urban migration and the lingering damage done by the civil war are partly to blame for the country's poor sanitation, the government's failure to address the issue in any meaningful way is also responsible for the continuing crisis. The government has only met around 30 percent of its own commitments in the area of sanitation, and it has consistently ignored this issue when drawing up the budget. The World Bank approved a $10 million credit in 2016 to put toward improvements in delivering clean water to the Liberian people, and other humanitarian groups have urged the Liberian government to create a separate ministry to focus on the country's water and sanitation needs. As it currently stands, sanitation is just one of many issues that come under the purview of the Ministry of Public Works, which is also responsible for the country's transportation and urban infrastructure. The Liberian government has not taken any action in this regard yet, suggesting that improving the country's sanitation network is not a top priority.

Water was a scarce resource during the civil war, and few improvements have been made since that time.

What this prioritization fails to account for is that poor sanitation and a lack of clean water will slow down efforts to improve many other aspects of Liberian society. Unclean water encourages the spread of diseases, including malaria and cholera, and the World Health Organization (WHO) estimates that up to 20 percent of the deaths in the country can be attributed to water or sanitation problems. These sick Liberians are also unable to work or contribute to the economy, slowing down economic growth (one estimate says that sanitation-related issues cost the Liberian economy $17.5 million a year).

The sanitation crisis also impacts education. Only 10 percent of schools have clean water running through them, forcing many students to leave school to buy water from street vendors. If they cannot afford to buy this water, they simply stay home. The learning process is also hindered by the

"Whenever we use the water from the wells in the community, our bodies get covered with rashes." —Kumba Korkor, Liberian businesswoman

Piles of garbage littered the streets of Monrovia in 2003, in the aftermath of the civil war.

fact that many students have no fresh water at home and are therefore required to help their families fetch water from sources that are sometimes miles away. The burden of fetching water disproportionately affects women and young girls, who are often taken out of school to help their mothers collect enough water to get the family through the day. Schools also lack clean restrooms—many have urine on the floor and overflowing toilets, preventing students from using them. This, too, has a disproportionate impact on female students, who are often forced to miss school entirely while they are menstruating. The net effect of these sanitation issues is to make it much more difficult for students to focus on their studies and learn effectively, hampering Liberia's overall progress in the field of education.

Until the government treats Liberia's poor sanitation infrastructure as the crisis that it is, the country will struggle to develop in more areas than one.

REFUSE COLLECTION

In the immediate aftermath of the civil war, a 2004 UN report observed that the collection of town and city waste had virtually stopped. As a result, residents were forced to either let refuse pile up in mountains of trash or dispose of it themselves through burning, causing dangerous air pollution. The ever-growing waste piles also led to public health issues, as water sources were polluted and drains became clogged with garbage, resulting

GARBAGE DISPOSAL

At the Red Light Market in Monrovia, piles of trash grew so large that they threatened to block the entrances. As the Christmas season approached in 2013, traders began to fear that the annual increase in customers would fail to materialize, as Liberians would be unable or unwilling to come inside. Frustrated by the lack of government action and fearful that they would lose a great deal of money, the traders eventually burned the refuse, producing a toxic blue haze.

in pools of stagnant water which bred mosquitoes and other disease carriers. The government partnered with several private organizations to dispose of the waste and has made real progress in getting the situation under control. About 30 percent of the country is now covered by trash collection services, and television and radio airwaves are informing citizens about the dangers posed by improper waste disposal.

In Liberia's slums, residents fish in sewage-polluted water.

Despite the improvements, uncollected waste continues to sit on the streets of Liberia's towns and cities, unless it is dumped into local rivers, swamps, or coastal waters. Hospitals often do not have any proper waste disposal systems, so medical waste—including syringes, bandages, and human matter—is thrown away in open sites with other town refuse. Industrial centers also pollute the surrounding air and water. The Mano and Saint John Rivers have become increasingly polluted from the dumping of industrial waste, including iron ore tailings, and coastal waters have become heavily polluted with oil residue, raw sewage, and wastewater.

INTERNET LINKS

http://www.fauna-flora.org/explore/liberia
Fauna and Flora International outlines the environmental challenges faced by Liberia, as well as the conservation programs and anti-deforestation efforts of the organization.

http://pygmyhippofoundation.org/about/sapo-national-park
This website discusses the history and geography of Sapo National Park.

LIBERIANS

Traditional tribal masks like this one are used in Liberian spiritual ceremonies.

S INCE LIBERIA'S BORDERS, LIKE those of virtually every other African nation, were arbitrarily decided based on the desires of American and European colonizers, the many ethnic groups that live within the country are only Liberian by accident of birth. In fact, since many ancestral tribal areas straddle the borders between Liberia and its neighbors, indigenous Liberians often have more of a linguistic and cultural connection to members of their own tribe in other countries than they do with their fellow Liberians.

Depending on what criteria one uses to define an ethnic group, there are between sixteen and twenty-eight unique peoples living in Liberia, in addition to the Americo-Liberians. Of these, just three—the Bassa, Dei, and Belleh—are found only in Liberia. All of the others exist in greater numbers in other countries.

Liberians are also distinguished from one another by the many religions that are practiced in the country, including Christianity, Islam, and traditional tribal faiths, as well as the divide that exists between urban and rural areas. Roughly 50 percent of the country's population lives in urban areas, where daily life tends to be more westernized. In rural areas, traditional village or tribal structure continues to be the predominant mode of existence.

As a result of this ethnic, religious, and geographic diversity, it is not easy to generalize about Liberians. A city dweller who is aware of being a descendant of a nineteenth-century family of freed slaves lives a very different life than a Muslim rice farmer from the Kissi tribe living in the interior of the country. Taken together, these divides have made it difficult for the residents of Liberia to forge a shared national identity, which has in turn played a part in the numerous violent conflicts that have riven Liberia in the past four decades.

DEMOGRAPHIC MAKEUP

The population of Liberia is about 4.3 million, or about 114 persons per square mile. The population is unevenly distributed, with most people living around Monrovia and in the stretch of land from Montserrado County to the Guinea border. The chief urban settlements include the coastal cities and towns of Monrovia, Buchanan, and Harper, as well as cities and towns of the interior, including Ganta, Gbarnga, and Kakata. There are about two thousand villages in the country, mostly in northwest and central Liberia, as well as some settlements just outside of Monrovia. By contrast, the southeastern forests are largely uninhabited. The population is increasingly moving from the countryside into the cities, as well as to enclaves around rubber plantations and iron mines. Despite this urbanization, the vast majority of the population continues to work in agriculture, though increasing numbers of Liberians are turning to industrial and service occupations. Indigenous Africans make up 95 percent of the population, while Americo-Liberians make up just 2.5 percent, and other groups, such as the Congos, make up the remaining 2.5 percent.

Liberia's population, which has increased by 1.3 million people in the last decade alone, is one of the fastest-growing in the world. Growing at a rate of 2.44 percent every year, this has produced a stark age disparity. Over 42 percent of the population is under fifteen years old, and another 19 percent is between ages fifteen and twenty-four; less than 8 percent of the

One area of noticeable progress in Liberia since the end of the civil war is the increase in life expectancy. Liberians now live an average of 59 years, with female life expectancy (60.8 years) higher than male life expectancy (57.3 years). While this number is still among the lowest in the world, it is a massive improvement for the country; in the first years after the civil war, life expectancy for Liberians hovered around an incredibly low 40.5 years of age.

population is older than fifty-five. The fertility rate currently stands at 4.6 children born per woman, resulting in large families with many dependents.

The population has increased for several reasons. With wages so low in Liberia, many families need several children to help with farm labor or otherwise provide financial support. The peace and stability that has been restored to Liberia has also played an important part in growing the population, though it has not been as vital as one might think; the population growth rate has actually declined over the past decade. Still, the cessation of hostilities as well as the improved health care now available in the country have increased life expectancy and decreased the infant mortality rate, which has dropped by 70 percent since 1990. There is also negligible emigration from Liberia, meaning that those born in the country tend to stay there.

ETHNIC GROUPS

The government of Liberia recognizes sixteen different tribes, although ethnolinguists put the number closer to thirty, based on language differences and cultural habits. The indigenous tribes can be broadly divided into three ethnolinguistic groups—that is, groups of people who share a common language and customs.

THE KWA-SPEAKING PEOPLES
The Kwa-speaking tribes include the Kru, Bassa, Dei, and Grebo. Their traditional homelands are the fertile plains extending along the sea from

In this old photograph, the Kru people take part in a traditional dance ceremony.

the Ivory Coast to Monrovia and beyond. The Kru are well known as accomplished seamen and traders. In the past, they dealt in slaves and wore tattoos on their foreheads to identify themselves as Kru in an effort to avoid enslavement. The Bassa live in central Liberia. They are one of the few tribes unique to the country, and they, like the other members of their language group, have migrated in large numbers to urban areas. The Grebo occupy the extreme southeast of the country.

Two small interior tribes, the Krahn and the Belleh, also speak a language related to these groups, although they are traditionally agriculturists and hunter-gatherers rather than seafarers.

THE MANDE-SPEAKING PEOPLES

The Mande speakers come from the north of the country and are indistinguishable from tribes of the same name in other West African countries.

ETHNIC GROUPS

The following list shows the largest ethnic groups in Liberia by percentage of total population.

Kpelle—20.3 percent

Bassa—13.4 percent

Grebo—10 percent

Gio—8 percent

Mano—7.9 percent

Kru—6 percent

Loma—5.1 percent

Kissi—4.8 percent

Gola—4.4 percent

Eight tribes of this group live in Liberia, each with different cultures and traditions. The Mende have a strong tradition of masked dancing, while the Loma have historically been soldiers in the Liberian army. The Mandingo, most of whom are Muslims, are traders. The Kpelle are the most traditional of these tribes, having remained hunter-gatherers and farmers. The Vai are a coastal group with a literary tradition. They, too, are predominantly Muslim, and most make their living through subsistence farming, fishing, and craftwork.

THE WEST ATLANTIC SPEAKERS

The West Atlantic speakers consist of a small group of tribes that most likely came to Liberia from the northwest. They are mainly rice farmers, and many of them are Muslim.

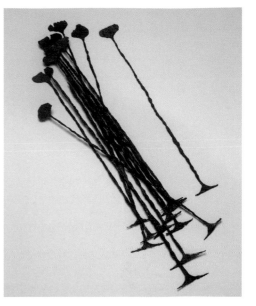

The Gola and Kissi belong to this group. The Kissi inhabit a belt of hills at the point where the borders of Guinea, Liberia, and Sierra Leone meet. They cultivate rice in natural marshland and grow yams, sweet potatoes, coffee, and kola nuts. Their huts are round and built of clay, and their villages are small. The Kissi make stone statues of their ancestors and are also famous for their currency, called "Kissi money"—small, twisted iron bars that are no longer in use.

Though usually grouped in bundles of twenty, Kissi money could also be used individually for smaller purchases.

THE RULING CLASS

Americo-Liberians, the country's wealthiest and most powerful ethnic group, are the descendants of the freed slaves and other African Americans who settled in Liberia in the nineteenth century. Though this group currently only makes up 2.5 percent of the population, Americo-Liberians had almost unilateral control over the country from its founding until the military coup in 1980. They are chiefly urban and educated, with a distinct class system encompassing a small, extremely wealthy elite that owns estates or businesses (numbering only about 1,500 people, or 3.3 percent of the total Americo-Liberian population), a middle class of clerical workers, and a lower class of poor manual laborers. Americo-Liberians are chiefly Christian, and

Members of the same ethnic group often share the same type of work. The Kru, for example, who live in the coastal towns, work mainly as sailors or as stevedores on the docks, although some have joined the teaching and medical professions, the civil service, and politics. They are organized into clan-like groups, and an organization called the Kru Corporation, founded in 1916, handles disputes between tribespeople and their employers.

though most live in the major towns or cities along the coast, some maintain homes in the country's interior.

Related to the Americo-Liberians are the Congo people, who also make up about 2.5 percent of the population. Barely distinguishable from Americo-Liberians, Congos are the descendants of freed slaves who were taken from slaving ships intercepted by the US Navy during the journey from Africa to the Caribbean. "Congo" has become a term of insult for all Americo-Liberians.

OTHER RESIDENTS

In addition to the Americo-Liberians and the various tribal groups that have always lived in Liberia, other groups have taken up residence in the country, on both a temporary and permanent basis. Though Liberia does not allow these residents to become citizens, they have nonetheless managed to become part of the social and cultural life of the country.

Many Ghanaians have settled in Liberia as semipermanent residents. They are chiefly people from the Fanti tribe, and they are traditionally fishermen who work along the coastal shores. Many of the Fanti have settled in Liberia's towns and cities, received an education, and have become office workers, adopting the urban lifestyle. The Fanti are largely literate, and there are as many people of Ghanaian extraction in Liberia as there are members of some of the country's smaller native tribes.

Another distinctive group found in Liberia is the Lebanese community. Arab traders settled extensively throughout West Africa, and Liberia was no exception. Even in small towns in Liberia, there are stores and restaurants

At one time, it was considered very fashionable in Liberia to wear clothes featuring portraits of famous African leaders as a design element.

run by Lebanese residents, who strive to maintain their unique culture.

Liberia is also home to approximately fifteen thousand refugees from the Ivory Coast, who fled their homeland in 2010 and 2011 as a result of post-election violence.

STYLES OF DRESS

When the early settlers came to Liberia from the United States, they emulated the dress of the wealthy plantation owners of the South, wearing frock coats, hats, and cravats. These days, most Liberians wear Western-style clothing that has been adapted for the heat and humidity of the tropical climate.

Traditional dress for women usually consists of a wide-necked blouse, called a *bubba*, and a full-length sarong, known as a *lappas*. Both garments are generally vivid in color. Most women also wear a headdress made from an elaborately tied scarf. Men typically wear loose, brightly colored shirts over Western-style cotton trousers.

When they take part in dance festivals, Liberians often cover themselves in white clay and wear long grass skirts, dyed and woven tunics, beads, and colorful headdresses.

NOTABLE LIBERIANS

Throughout the years, many people have established themselves within Liberia's history. These are a few who have helped the country become what it is today.

Liberian women in traditional dress; note the head scarf and the *lappas* of the woman on the right.

Ellen Johnson Sirleaf's long career includes work in Liberia, the United States, and other nations in Africa.

ELLEN JOHNSON SIRLEAF is Africa's first elected female president. She took office in 2006. Born in Monrovia on October 29, 1938, Johnson Sirleaf is of Gola and Kru ancestry. Her grandfather was a renowned tribal chief, and her father was the first indigenous African to sit in Liberia's national legislature. She attended high school in Liberia and college in the United States, eventually earning a master's degree in public administration from Harvard University in 1971. Returning to Liberia, Johnson Sirleaf served in President Tolbert's administration, eventually becoming minister of finance in 1979. This position proved to be tragically short-lived, as Tolbert's government was overthrown a year later.

Over the next two decades, Johnson Sirleaf made occasional forays into Liberian politics but spent most of her time in exile from Liberia. She was imprisoned briefly by Samuel Doe for criticizing his administration, and she was later threatened with legal persecution after she placed second in the 1997 presidential election, which was won by Charles Taylor. Johnson Sirleaf had initially backed Taylor in his effort to retake control of the country but parted ways with him in the early days of the civil war. During her time away from Liberia, Johnson Sirleaf worked for several different banks in Africa and the United States. She also worked for the United Nations Development Program (UNDP). This helped make her a strong candidate for the presidency in 2005, when she ran on a platform of unity, anticorruption, and a promise to return foreign investment to Liberia.

Her administration succeeded in the latter goal to the tune of $16 billion, though corruption has continued to plague the Liberian government. Despite that, Liberia has remained at peace, and a degree of stability has been achieved. For her efforts in rebuilding Liberia and protecting women's rights, Johnson Sirleaf was one of three recipients of the 2011 Nobel Peace Prize. She has also received numerous other honors and awards, including the Presidential Medal of Freedom in 2007. Johnson Sirleaf left office in 2018.

LEYMAH GBOWEE was also selected by the Nobel Committee to receive the 2011 Peace Prize, for her work mobilizing and organizing women to bring Liberia's civil war to an end. Born in 1972, Gbowee's education was disrupted by the civil

Leymah Gbowee's nonviolent resistance movement helped bring the Liberian civil war to an end.

war, which forced her to flee to Ghana with her family. Returning to Liberia to work as a trauma counselor for former child soldiers, Gbowee went on to found the Women of Liberia Mass Action for Peace, an organization of women from different ethnic and religious backgrounds. Together, the women fasted, prayed, and picketed at markets and in front of government buildings, becoming a presence that could not be ignored. Gbowee and her group also followed Charles Taylor to peace talks in Ghana, refusing to let anyone leave the meeting until a deal was struck. When Taylor's security forces attempted to remove Gbowee, she threatened to remove her clothes, an act which, according to traditional beliefs, would bring a great curse of misfortune upon the men. Gbowee and the women she mobilized were instrumental in bringing the civil war to an end, and in the years since that time, Gbowee has launched several other humanitarian organizations aimed at educating and empowering girls and women. In addition to the Nobel Prize, Gbowee was honored with the John F. Kennedy Profile in Courage Award in 2009, and was chosen to carry the Olympic flag during the opening ceremonies of the 2012 Olympic Games in London.

Charles Taylor appears in court in 2006 to plead not guilty to crimes against humanity. His trial would begin the following year.

CHARLES TAYLOR is the former president of Liberia, and his invasion of the country at the head of the National Patriotic Front of Liberia (NPFL) in 1989 began a civil war that lasted until 2003. Born in 1948 to a family of Americo-Liberians, Taylor was educated in the United States before returning to his homeland in the 1980s, where he took up a position in Samuel Doe's government. His job put him in charge of most of Liberia's budget, and Taylor took advantage of his situation to embezzle $900,000 and flee back to the United States. Taylor eventually returned to Africa under mysterious circumstances, which he alleges involved the US government giving him training in an effort to overthrow Doe's regime.

Taylor was elected president of Liberia in 1997, but his administration quickly lost any support it may have had when it became clear that he was involved in war crimes in neighboring Sierra Leone. As the civil war resumed in Liberia and it became increasingly likely that he would lose power, the eccentric Taylor began a series of bizarre efforts to maintain his position. He adopted the middle name Ghankay, in an effort to appeal to indigenous Africans, and showed up to a prayer meeting dressed all in white to beg forgiveness for the war crimes he insisted he did not commit. At the peace talks in 2003, Taylor arrived in full combat gear and forced his bodyguards to jog alongside his car during his trip from the airport, as a demonstration of his strength.

These attempts to escape justice predictably failed, and Taylor was forced out of office in 2003. At the same time, he was indicted by the United Nations, formally accused of crimes against humanity in Sierra Leone. He was arrested in 2006 after a chase in which he attempted to flee in a disguised diplomatic car with huge sacks of cash, and his trial began in 2007 in the Netherlands. Among other things, Taylor was accused of helping recruit child soldiers to fight in the civil war in Sierra Leone and selling weapons to warlords in exchange for diamonds. The trial finally ended in 2011, and Taylor was found guilty of committing war crimes. In 2012, he was sentenced to fifty years in prison, which he is currently serving in the United Kingdom.

INTERNET LINKS

https://www.nobelprize.org/nobel_prizes/peace/laureates/2011/ johnson_sirleaf-facts.html
The Nobel Prize committee prepared a brief biographical summary of Ellen Johnson Sirleaf before she was awarded the Peace Prize in 2011. The site also contains a link to the lecture Johnson Sirleaf delivered when she accepted the award.

http://www.rscsl.org/Taylor.html
This site provides a summary and timeline of Charles Taylor's trial for war crimes, held in the Netherlands.

LIFESTYLE

Though some areas of Monrovia have been modernized, much of the city is still without electricity or running water.

7

FOR DECADES, LIBERIA APPEARED TO be one of the most stable nations on the African continent. Beneath the surface of that stability, however, lurked the deep divides and inequalities that have always plagued the country. Those divides were thrust to the forefront during the years of military dictatorship and civil war, and have continued to draw sharp distinctions between Liberians in the years since the peace.

These are not only differences of religion or ethnicity, but divisions between the tribal life of the villages and the westernized life of the cities, and between the rich and the poor. The inequalities inherent to life in Liberia are self-reinforcing and generational, and have severely hampered the country's ability to rebuild in the fifteen years since the end of the civil war. Overcrowded cities, insufficient health care, and poor educational opportunities are a regular feature of life for most Liberians. For those living outside of the cities, food insecurity and potentially harmful traditional practices represent further sources of stress. Life is incredibly hard for virtually all Liberians, and while the improvements made over the last decade have undoubtedly been important, they have still not gone anywhere near far enough. Until the government commits to serious, properly funded programs to improve living conditions in the country, most Liberians will struggle simply to survive.

"During Ebola time, you couldn't even visit your friends. Even in your own house, you can't touch anyone. You couldn't hug your kids. People were very afraid." —Levi Learwellie, villager

THE CITIES

American visitors to Monrovia in 1980 might have been forgiven for believing themselves to still be in the United States. The currency was the US dollar, the police officers wore second-hand New York Police Department summer uniforms, and signs outside the larger towns announced their names as New Georgia, Maryland, and Louisiana. On Saturday nights the nightclubs and bars were lit up, while on Sundays Baptist choirs could be heard. These legacies of Monrovia's founding by "repatriated" black Americans were largely wiped out by the civil war and the subsequent peace; the Liberian dollar replaced the US dollar, the police received their own uniforms, and the once vibrant city went dark.

In Liberia's cities, open-air markets serve food and other goods to the country's residents.

Monrovia is a physically small capital, with an area of only about 5 square miles (13 sq km). It is also the home of 1.3 million people. This overcrowding has overwhelmed the infrastructure and resources of the city, which is now in a near-permanent state of disrepair. Housing is cramped and congested, and there is almost no sanitation system to speak of. Metal roofs are often rusted and brown, mold and mildew grows freely, and roads and buildings, even when refurbished, quickly break down from the sheer amount of use they are given. The city's streets are a nightmare for motorists to navigate. They are incredibly narrow, and most drivers have almost no regard for traffic laws. Official vehicles blow past with sirens blaring, taxis cut off other automobiles with reckless abandon, and cars frequently make sudden stops in the middle of the road. Most of Monrovia still lacks electricity (to which only 10 percent of Liberia's entire population has access), and the government's promise to restore electric power to the city has become a grim joke for most of its residents. Supporting themselves in any way they can, many Monrovians sell goods at markets, while others try to sell gum or candy to people stuck in traffic. Some, disabled in the civil war, simply beg along the streets. At night, Monrovians frequently go to the bars and nightclubs that are connected to the electric grid, as they are among the few places at which it is possible to relax and have fun in the city.

> ## COSMOPOLITAN MONROVIA
>
> *Despite the many challenges it faces, Monrovia remains the cultural and educational center of Liberia. The city is home to museums, a zoo, and several colleges and universities.*

Cities and towns in Liberia are often visually expressive of the nation's wealth inequality, as those in extreme poverty live in close proximity to the wealthiest individuals in the country. This produces a rather interesting mix of architecture, as dilapidated mansions and bungalows in the style of the American South are often found alongside modern high-rise buildings, which are in turn built within walking distance of traditional African huts and poverty-stricken shantytowns. At a glance, this affords swift insight into the varying lifestyles present in Liberia.

Beyond the cities of the coast, other towns and cities have developed in the interior of the country along the major routes to large mining and farming estates. The people living in these cities tend to be young and disproportionately male, as young men typically migrate from rural areas to the cities in search of work. Two-story concrete housing blocks predominate in the modern parts of these cities, while older homes are rectangular and one-storied, with their walls made of plaited mats or mud and wattle, with tin roofs.

THE EDUCATION SYSTEM

In the early years of settlement by Americo-Liberians, education for the settlers' children was considered to be of paramount importance. Americo-Liberian children were educated in locally established schools for entrance into professions such as law, theology, and medicine. After elementary school, they usually went to the United States, Europe, or neighboring African countries to complete their education. No provision was made for indigenous children to go to school, and until 1961, the vast majority of children in the country were only educated by isolated missionary groups. A

Liberian students
attend class
in Monrovia.

national education system was finally established in the 1960s, which extended schooling to the indigenous population. This system included six years of elementary school, three years of junior high school, and three years of high school. By the late 1960s, 50 percent of schools were financed and run by the government; the rest were privately run facilities and mission schools.

This system lasted until the civil war in 1989, which did tremendous damage to educational progress in Liberia. Approximately 80 percent of the schools in the country were looted, damaged, or destroyed during the conflict, and an entire generation was denied the opportunity to get any kind of steady education. Less than half of the country is literate, and two-thirds of the current working population has a primary education or less; that number rises to 80 percent for working women, who are typically less educated than men.

Under President Ellen Johnson Sirleaf, Liberia made only limited progress toward rebuilding its education system. The majority of Liberian children are still not attending schools, for a variety of reasons. Some children do not have access to transport to the nearest school, while others lack the financial means to attend (though primary and secondary school are theoretically free, families are expected to cover the costs of students' uniforms, books, and other supplies). Some kids are also expected to help their parents with household chores or other work, and are kept out of school as a result. The children who are not in school are overwhelmingly rural, poor, and female.

Enrollment is not the only problem facing Liberia's education system, however. For students who are attending school, academic progress is hampered by overcrowded classrooms, poorly trained teachers, and environments that are not conducive to learning. Many students do not have electricity at home, nor are their parents educated enough to help them with their studies, preventing them from doing any schoolwork outside of the classroom. Older students who move to cities to continue their education at nearby schools become vulnerable to predators, particularly teenage girls, who are often sexually exploited by teachers or landlords in return for grades or money. The Ebola outbreak in 2014 also stifled student progress, as over four thousand schools were forced to close for six months while the crisis was being dealt with. As a result of these challenges, Liberian students lag behind most other African students in academic outcomes. Only 49 percent of Liberian children are literate, and only 78 percent continue with their schooling past primary school. In 2013, twenty-five thousand Liberian students took the University of Liberia's entrance exam—none passed.

The University of Liberia opened in 1863 and is the largest public institute of higher learning in the country.

In response, the Liberian Ministry of Education partnered with several international organizations, including the United States Agency for International Development (USAID), to improve the education system. Reforms included strengthening teacher certification standards, rebuilding curricula, and improving access to schools for girls and other Liberians who have historically been excluded. The government also experimented with privatization, turning over dozens of schools to charter school networks. The results from these schools were dismal initially, however, as teachers read prepared scripts from cheap tablets and barely interacted with their students. Some public school teachers, who went on strike when the charter school scheme was first proposed, pointed out that if the government had used the money given to these private companies to raise teacher salaries, many teachers would no longer have to work second jobs and could devote more time and energy to their students. This would achieve equal, if not better, educational outcomes, and would benefit Liberians, rather than a foreign corporation.

Further education is largely provided by the University of Liberia in Monrovia, the largest public college in the country, as well as Cuttington University in Suakoko, and the William V. S. Tubman University in Harper. There are also several teacher-training colleges and a school for paramedics in Monrovia. USAID has partnered with the University of Liberia and Cuttington University to expand access as well as improve the quality of agriculture and engineering programs, two of the most relevant fields of study for the country.

In Liberia, 630,000 people (14 percent of the population) do not have enough to eat. This is a problem that is worse in rural areas and among the poorest individuals in the country, including refugees. A quarter of families in Liberia spend 65 percent of their income on food alone, and 18 percent are forced to rely on emergency coping strategies, like theft or begging, to get enough to eat. This problem stems from the decreased agricultural production that resulted from the civil war, during which most farmers only grew enough food for their own families. Though production has increased since the war ended, it has not reached the levels at which it once existed. Most farmers still only grow what they need, and livestock farming is also too small-scale to meet public demand. Liberia therefore imports most of its food, and in a country where most people make less than a dollar a day, the price of the imported food is more than some can afford. Humanitarian organizations, including the World Food Programme (WFP), are working to combat the crisis posed by food insecurity by providing food to Ebola survivors and orphans, giving free school meals and take-home food to students who maintain a steady attendance rate, and participating in programs in which food is given to people in exchange for their work on infrastructure projects.

Larger villages, often evolving along the roads built by foreign companies or along old trading routes, are more sophisticated. They have rectangular huts with corrugated iron roofs, and they hold a grand market day when people from the smaller villages congregate and spend the whole day trading. Mandingo traders travel around the various village markets, which are intentionally held on different days.

SECRET SOCIETIES

Most rural Liberians are members of some kind of secret society. Secret societies have a long history in Liberia, dating back to the eighteenth century. The two major ones are the Sande (SAN-day) and Poro (POH-roh), secret societies for women and men, respectively. Secrecy is taken seriously by members of these societies, and little is known about exactly what happens within them. Bush schools are held every year to induct young people, and as people pass through the various stages in the society, they learn new rituals and lore, with the overall goal of deterring antisocial behavior or beliefs and building solidarity within the tribe.

The Poro schools teach boys practical skills such as building liana (a type of tree) bridges, handling wives, and building houses, but they also teach tribal law, correct behavior toward elders, and secrets of religion. Ritual tattooing and scarring are sometimes part of the course. The Sande schools traditionally taught girls about cooking and the mysteries of marriage, childbirth, and witchcraft, but are said to have become less magic-oriented in recent years. Girls are usually forced to undergo female genital cutting (FGC) as part of their initiation into the society.

The old, elite Americo-Liberian families also had a powerful males-only secret society—the Ancient, Free, and Accepted Masonic Lodge of Liberia. The society was founded in 1867, and by 1980, when it was decimated in the coup, it had about seventeen branches in Liberia. Virtually all of the nation's social and political leaders were members, and the lodge had a powerful influence on government decisions. The Masons were bitterly resented by the newly emerging young professionals of tribal origin in the 1970s and 1980s. There was also a women's version of the lodge—the Order of the Eastern Star of Africa.

INTERNET LINKS

http://www1.wfp.org/countries/liberia
The World Food Programme outlines the crisis posed by food insecurity in Liberia and details the initiatives undertaken to combat it.

http://www.who.int/countries/lbr/en
The World Health Organization's profile of Liberia includes statistics about the country's health-care outcomes and the latest health-related news from Liberia and the West African region.

RELIGION

More than 85 percent of Liberians identify as Christians, making church services like this one common throughout the country.

8

"Belief that all power has its origin in the invisible world, where God and spirits dwell, is a constant of Liberian history." —Stephen Ellis, anthropologist and historian

AS BEFITS A NATION SETTLED BY different groups at different times, Liberia is home to numerous religions. In addition to Christianity and Islam, there are also several indigenous tribal faiths, unique to particular ethnic groups. In a 2008 census, 85.6 percent of Liberians identified themselves as Christians, 12.2 percent as Muslims, and 0.6 percent as adherents to traditional faiths.

While this may lead one to assume that the country is Christian, it is important to note that many native African tribes have blended elements of Christianity or Islam with their traditional beliefs, producing a hybrid faith. Though individuals from these tribes may identify as Christian, many of their beliefs and cultural practices have their origin in the traditional religions of their ancestors and would be unfamiliar to Christians of Europe or the United States.

The oldest forms of religious belief in Liberia are the indigenous religions, of which animism is a common aspect. People who follow these religions believe in a supreme god, but they usually experience spiritual power through everyday objects or beings that are thought to be endowed with supernatural elements. Islam was introduced to West Africa by caravan merchants crossing the Sahara Desert during the eleventh century and was spread to present-day Liberia by certain African tribes, particularly the Mandingo. Christianity is the most

Believed to contain magical forces that will guide and protect a particular individual, totems are objects of great significance among certain indigenous faiths, especially within the Kpelle tribe. A totem can be a specific species of animal or variety of plant, or something as simple as a rock. Appearances of an individual's totem are taken as an omen, and people with the same totem consider themselves kin. Most children are given a plant totem at birth, though fathers can pass their totems on to their sons, and mothers to their daughters.

recently introduced religion, only arriving in appreciable numbers with the immigrants from the United States and the Caribbean in the early nineteenth century. Missionaries encouraged the spread of Christianity into the interior of the country throughout the nineteenth and twentieth centuries, and Christian schools were often the only source of education for indigenous African children.

Though religion represents another clear divide between Liberians, religiously motivated violence has not been a major source of conflict in the country. Differing religious traditions may sharpen the distinctions between particular tribal groups, but ethnicity has historically been the deepest source of discord among Liberians. Discrimination on the basis of religion is outlawed in Liberia, and the country is among the most religiously tolerant in all of Africa.

INDIGENOUS FAITHS

The oldest religions in Liberia are the animistic faiths of the country's native tribes. Although the different groups' religious beliefs vary, the animistic religions of Liberia do have some features in common. Animists believe in a spiritual world where their surroundings—be they living or nonliving—are imbued with life and the power to cause harm or good. All objects encountered must therefore be treated with reverence. Objects can also be called upon to help the individual, usually through the aid of someone called a *zoe* (ZOH), the animist equivalent of both a priest and doctor.

Animists believe in three gods—the creator, the ancestor, and the nature spirit. Particular emphasis is placed on the ancestor and the nature spirit, which represent different aspects of the spiritual world. Followers of indigenous religions place great value on the spirits of their ancestors, which are believed to affect their own lives. Individuals of special importance are worshipped not only by their relatives but also by other members of the village. As time passes, older spirits fade away into a group that, though still recognized in worship, is thought to have less power than the spirits of the recently deceased. A nature spirit is the spirit of a particular rock, tree, or river that animists believe has the power to affect the lives of those living nearby. Animists give the object a name and try to appease it with sacrifices. A spirit may also make an appearance in its "true form," in which case viewers can be harmed or benefited, depending on how the spirit is treated.

This mask, used by medicine men among the Gio tribe of Liberia, depicts a spiritual being with the eyes of a man and the mouth of a crocodile.

WITCHCRAFT

As part of their belief in the power of spirits to bring about earthly change, animists offer gifts and carry out rituals in an effort to appease the supernatural forces around them. This practice is called magic or witchcraft, and it is carried out by *zoes*. These specialists use herbs or animal tissue (including, in some cases, human flesh) to create substances that are believed to have medicinal and spiritual properties. The medicines can be eaten, carried as an amulet, or even hidden near a particular person in order to affect him or her in some way. While some medicines are legitimate herbal remedies, others are purely faith-based.

ISLAM IN LIBERIA

Though Islam is not as widespread as Christianity, it is still the religion of more than one in ten Liberians. Coming to West Africa through early caravan traders, it was spread around the region by indigenous tribes. In Liberia, the first tribe to adopt and spread Islam was the Mandingo, members of which

Though most urbanized Liberians claim that they no longer believe in magic, there have been cases in recent history of powerful political figures appealing to its protections. For instance, when President Samuel Doe was assassinated in 1990 by Prince Johnson's rebel group, he was left to die with his arms tied. This was done based on a traditional belief that, if he were freed, his spirit would be released and could gain power over another body.

are approximately 90 percent Muslim today. The Vai have also converted to Islam in large numbers, as have other tribes, including the Gola, Mende, Kissi, and Gbandi.

Islam originated in Arabia in the seventh century CE and follows the teachings of the Prophet Muhammad. Muslims believe in one god, referred to as Allah, in angels who bring his word to the people, and in the twenty-eight prophets who received Allah's message, among them Jesus Christ, Moses, and other figures familiar to Judaism and Christianity. Most Liberian Muslims belong to the Sunni sect of Islam. The Sunnis acknowledge the first four caliphs as the rightful successors to the Prophet Muhammad. Shia Muslims, who believe that Muhammad was succeeded by his son-in-law Ali, are a minority among Muslims in Liberia, though the country's Lebanese community is primarily Shiite.

CHRISTIANITY IN LIBERIA

The first Christians to settle in Liberia were the former slaves and free blacks from the United States and the Caribbean. Primarily of the Methodist and Baptist branches of Christianity, these first settlers owed their passage to Africa, in part, to Christianity, as religious beliefs had been a primary motivating factor for many of the Americans who came to support colonization. As the principal denominations of the Americo-Liberian ruling class, Methodists and Baptists were able to exert disproportionate influence over Liberia for the next 150 years. Typical religious services during the early years of settlement included evangelical revival meetings, at which testimonies would be given

In an example of the blending between Christianity and indigenous Liberian religions, *zoes* among some native tribes endow protective amulets with holy power by inscribing them with verses from the Bible.

and hymns would be sung. Over time, services grew more subdued and formal.

Other churches arrived later. The Roman Catholic Church set up missions among the Kru, Grebo, and Krahn, gaining many converts from among those tribes. The Lutheran Church, meanwhile, focused its missionary activity on the Kpelle and Loma peoples. The Episcopal Church became a prestigious organization, adopted by many among the educated elite, as well as by tribal students at Cuttington University, an Episcopal institution.

In addition to the mainstream denominations, other Christian churches have emerged that have their origins in Africa. Congregations of these newer churches tend to be manual workers with little formal education, and they are also usually ethnically homogenous. By contrast, members of mainstream churches are more likely to be wealthy, literate, and cosmopolitan. Indigenous African churches include the Liberian Assemblies of God, which has missions among the urban Kru, as well as the Church of the Lord. Also known as the Aladura Church, it originated in Nigeria and spread throughout West Africa. Services at the Aladura Church feature faith healing, African music, and an overall lively atmosphere.

Liberia's Muslim communities practice their faith in the country's mosques.

INTERNET LINKS

http://www.innovateus.net/innopedia/what-animism
This website provides a brief overview of the diverse beliefs and practices of animist religions.

http://www.state.gov/j/drl/rls/irf/religiousfreedom/index.htm?year=2015&dlid=256039
This report, compiled by the US State Department, discusses religious freedom in Liberia.

LANGUAGE

The many indigenous languages native to Liberia can occasionally make interpersonal communication difficult, and most Liberians speak multiple languages.

9

LIBERIA HAS AN EXTREMELY COMPLEX system of languages. The country's official language is English, but there are more than thirty indigenous languages spoken by Liberia's many tribes. These languages can be divided into three main groups, based on their linguistic origins: the Mande, which is the most common; the Kwa; and the West Atlantic, or Mel. Some tribes, such as the Vai, have also adopted Arabic. In addition to these languages, various forms of "pidgin English," regional dialects adapted from English, are also spoken around the country.

As a result of the many languages spoken in Liberia, communication can be rather difficult. Intertribal communication is often made through a common root language or pidgin English, and most Liberians are multilingual. The majority of the native languages exist only in oral form, however; written correspondence is generally done entirely in English.

THE OFFICIAL LANGUAGE

English is the official government language of Liberia. It is used in politics, education, newspapers, radio, and television. Though it is the

"People assume (Americo-Liberians) brought English to Liberia. But in fact, English was already there—the West African variety, pidgin English."
—John Singler, linguist at New York University

Liberian newspapers are written in English, the country's official language.

mother tongue of only a small percentage of Liberians, it is spoken in one form or another as a second language by the majority of the population. Liberian English differs from the English spoken in other parts of Africa in that it is derived from American English, rather than the British English introduced in the countries that were once British colonies. For example, in Nigeria you would buy "biscuits" in a "shop"; in Liberia, you would buy "cookies" in a "store." Names in Liberia are primarily European in origin because the former slaves and free blacks who settled in the country and came to dominate it politically generally had non-African names. Indigenous African names have become more common over the last couple decades.

In addition to the standard American English of broadcasting, government, and international business, there are also many pidgin varieties. The English of the Americo-Liberians, many of whom spoke an African American Creole form of English when they arrived, evolved into a dialect much closer to the country's indigenous languages than the pidgin tongues of neighboring countries. In Monrovia there are many pidgins, each one influenced by the mother tongue of an individual tribe. In some cases—for example, the Monrovian pidgin called Kepama—the pidgin has *become* the mother tongue and is spoken more regularly than the original language.

THE INDIGENOUS LANGUAGES

The dozens of languages native to Liberia are grouped into three families: the Mande, the Kwa, and the West Atlantic. None of these language groups is unique to Liberia; each is spoken in several other countries in West Africa. The Mande languages, for example, extend into Mali, Guinea, the Ivory Coast, and Sierra Leone. In Liberia, they are spoken by eight tribes, most of which live in the north and east of the country. Not all Mande speakers can understand one another.

Although it is acknowledged that Liberians speak a form of American English, American kwi (KWEE, pidgin for "foreigners") in Monrovia would have a hard time understanding what the average person on the street was saying. Many of the final sounds of words are not pronounced in Liberian English, and a great many others are slurred. For example, many words have the suffix "o," so "cheap" becomes "cheap-o." There are also some differences in usage that might be confusing. If you wanted to congratulate someone, you would say "thank you!" rather than "congratulations!" Meanwhile, buses, cars, and motorbikes—in fact, any wheeled vehicle—are all called "cars."

There are many variations of the Kwa language, most of them not spoken in Liberia. Kwa speakers inhabit the coastline and the south of the country. Typical of the Kwa languages is the use of tone to give context to a word. The closeness of Kwa languages can be seen in the word for "water," which is *ni* (NEE) in the languages of the Bassa, Kru, and Kuwaa. Similarly, the word for "tree" is *chu* (CHU) in all three languages.

The West Atlantic speakers are the Gola and Kissi of Liberia and Sierra Leone. These tribes, the oldest inhabitants of Liberia, live in the north. Their languages form part of a group of twenty-three languages spoken around West Africa, the most important of which is Fulani. Like the Kwa languages, these tongues use tone to indicate meaning.

INTERTRIBAL COMMUNCIATION

The main intertribal language in Liberia is pidgin English, which is commonly spoken in most cities and towns. On the more local level, particularly in certain villages and rural areas, common tribal languages are used. In northern and western Liberia, where all three language groups exist in close proximity to one another, most people are at least bilingual, and in a large enough group, every individual can be understood by at least one other.

In regions like this—particularly the area northwest of Monrovia—some indigenous languages are disappearing as the people adopt not English but

In Weasua, a small town in the northwest of Grand Cape Mount County, it is claimed that you can hear every indigenous Liberian language spoken.

TALKING DRUMS

Common throughout West Africa, talking drums were an early form of communication in Liberia. These instruments are shaped like an hourglass, with skins on both ends that are connected by tightly stretched rawhide cords. An expert drum player can alter the sound of the drum by stretching or releasing these cords, thus creating a series of tones similar to the tonal languages of Liberia. Drummers would learn a standardized series of beats and tones, which became a kind of Morse code that corresponded to the pattern of actual words. The sound of the drums carried over long distances, and messages could be relayed over hundreds of miles in a very short time. A talking-drum player made this music his life's work.

another native language. The Dei, for example, have taken up the Vai language at home as well as in business. Malinke (mah-LINK-ee), the language spoken by the Mandingo, has become a lingua franca (or common language) because of the Mandingoes' traditional role as traveling traders.

In some unusual cases, the speakers of one language can understand another language, but cannot in turn be understood by speakers of that language. For example, the Gbee speakers of Nimba County can understand the language of the Bassa, but cannot be understood by them.

WRITTEN COMMUNICATION

In many cases, the first written forms of native African languages came about through the efforts of missionaries, particularly Lutherans, who created written alphabets in order to teach the Bible to the tribes. In Liberia, this was not the case. The vast number of subdialects in the country made the work of the missionaries very difficult, since a script understandable to one group would often make no sense to another group in a neighboring village.

A script was developed for the Kpelle, and alphabets were created for some other languages, but the first usable written language was invented by the Vai for their own language. In the early nineteenth century, a script developed by a Vai named Dualu Bukele came into common usage by the tribe and became the basis for written versions of other languages. The

During World War II, German intelligence officers used the Vai script to pass coded messages.

script is not an alphabet, but rather a syllabary. It has about 240 characters, each standing for a different vowel/consonant combination. Originally used to keep records of births, deaths, and marriages, the script is now used only by elderly men and is passed on to interested scholars.

PORTUGUESE INFLUENCES

Early explorers of the region that became Liberia included the Portuguese, who gave names to some of the country's geographic features. The Mesurado River, for example, was named by the Portuguese and means "measured" or "quiet," probably because the mouth of the river is calm. The Gallinas River has a Portuguese name that means "hens."

The names of the Saint John and Saint Paul Rivers have been anglicized, but they were also originally Portuguese. The name of the Cess River comes from the Portuguese word *cestor*, meaning "basket" (probably after the basket-wielding fisherwomen the explorers encountered there). The name for the region of Liberia bordering on the Gulf of Guinea—the Grain Coast— also comes from the Portuguese, who named it for the grains of melegueta pepper they found growing there.

The Vai script, created in the early 1800s, is one of the only written systems of communication among Liberia's indigenous inhabitants.

INTERNET LINKS

https://www.alsintl.com/resources/languages/Liberian/
This website offers a succinct overview of the development of the pidgin English spoken in Liberia, in addition to further information about the country's history.

http://www.languagesgulper.com/eng/Mande.html
The Mande language group is profiled here. Not only is its grammatical structure broken down, but its origins and relationships to other African languages are also examined.

ARTS

This painting is displayed on the side of a building in Monrovia.

A S THE LIBERIAN GOVERNMENT HAS focused on rebuilding the country's political and economic infrastructure over the last fifteen years, the arts have been reflective of similar rejuvenation in the country's social and cultural traditions. Though the poverty experienced by most Liberians has prevented widespread participation in the arts, the country nevertheless has a rich history of literature, music, and pictorial art. Liberian art draws inspiration from both African and Western sources, and offers insight into the unique experiences of Liberians in both urban and rural areas.

LITERARY TRADITIONS

Traditional literature arrived in Liberia with the ancestors of the Kpelle and Kru tribes as they migrated across Africa from Sudan. They brought with them stories, parables, and proverbs, as well as histories and legends about their ancestors' lives. Together, these stories represented the collected wisdom and spiritual values of the tribe, which were passed

Guanya Pau: A Story of an African Princess, published in 1891, is the earliest surviving English-language novel written by a black African. Its author, Joseph Jeffrey Walters, was born in Liberia among the Vai tribe.

down to succeeding generations by the fireside, in the bush schools, and in the meeting place of the village, where festivals celebrating the ancient stories were held. Although most tribes had no written form of language, the stories survived, and indeed they grew in the telling as new storytellers contributed fresh ideas. While anthropologists in the last century have recorded many of these stories, others have faded away as the oral tradition has died out among the increasing numbers of Liberians who are moving from the villages to the cities.

When the freed slaves arrived in Africa in the early nineteenth century, they brought with them a different literary and cultural tradition. The customs and cultural practices of slaves in the United States and the Caribbean were unique, as they drew on elements from both Africa and the slaveholding powers. When these individuals were resettled in Africa, they brought this amalgamated culture with them, and it underwent a further wave of cultural diffusion when it intermingled with indigenous Liberian cultural traditions.

The Americo-Liberians were mostly able to read and write, and their literary background was in the hymns and religious texts of Christianity. Their early literary efforts reflected this heritage, as religious poetry and pulpit orations were the dominant form of literature for the early settlers. These texts were united around the common theme of religious salvation in hard times and were indicative of the early settlers' reliance on God and Christianity during their first difficult years of settlement.

MODERN LIBERIAN LITERATURE

As Americo-Liberian and indigenous African culture gradually shared ideas with one another over the course of the twentieth century, a new Liberian literature emerged. The country's most famous novel, *Murder in the Cassava Patch* by Bai T. Moore, was published in 1968. It is a novel about forbidden relationships and social taboos, and is required reading for most Liberian students. Another novel frequently assigned in schools is Wilton Sankawulo's *Why Nobody Knows When He Will Die*. Sankawulo's clear and straightforward writing realistically depicted the ambitions, mistakes, and flaws of characters that were recognizably Liberian, in settings that reflected the country's changing culture and the differences between its urban and rural citizens. He is generally considered the most significant writer in Liberia's modern history. He also served briefly as chair of the Council of State, the interim government, during the civil war in the 1990s. Other important writers in modern-day Liberia include Robert Brown, a lecturer at the University of Liberia who also writes novels and short stories; Ophelia Lewis; Stephanie Horton; Robert Sesay; and K-Moses Nagbe.

Ophelia Lewis is the author of several books, short stories, poems, and the memoir *My Dear Liberia.*

Since the death of Wilton Sankawulo in 2009, Liberia has yet to have another writer break through and gain some degree of international renown. Part of the reason for this is financial—without government investment in, and encouragement of, the arts, it is difficult to build a national literary scene, like those that exist in other African nations. Past government censorship of works of art that were too sharply critical of the government or the Americo-Liberian class also hampered the development of a vibrant literary community. The country's school system is a further obstacle, as many students are not able to receive enough education (for a variety of reasons) to enable them to write. Liberia's diversity of languages also plays a role in limiting the growth of written literature, as many languages do not have a written form, and the speakers of those languages are not familiar enough with English to use it to record their stories.

Liberia's writers have attempted to band together to spread their work, forming collective networks and journals to meet one another and share their writings, but these efforts have had little impact outside of the country. *Kwee: Liberian Literary Magazine* is the current incarnation of these endeavors. It publishes poems, short stories, and essays submitted by a variety of Liberian writers.

EDWARD WILMOT BLYDEN

Perhaps the most famous writer to ever live and work in Liberia, Edward Wilmot Blyden was born in the US Virgin Islands in August 1832. His parents were free blacks, and he was taught how to read and write at an early age—this was at a time when most blacks in the Virgin Islands were illiterate slaves. Moving to Venezuela in 1842, Blyden observed that free blacks in the South American country were doing almost the same work as the slaves in the Virgin Islands. This made Blyden conscious of the limited opportunities afforded blacks, a fact that was further emphasized to him when he was denied admittance to an American theological college on account of his race. Blyden instead accepted an offer to teach in Liberia, where he lived for most of his life. As an educator, newspaper editor, and ordained minister, Blyden fought against the myths of black inferiority that had been rampant in Europe and the United States for centuries. He argued for black equality around the world, and he pushed back against the Americo-Liberian ruling elite of the country, encouraging other blacks to immigrate to Liberia. Blyden authored several books, including Africa for the Africans *in 1872, as well as numerous articles in which he set out his arguments. After a failed run for the Liberian presidency in 1885, Blyden went into self-imposed exile in Sierra Leone, where he died in 1912. Since his passing and continuing today, however, his words have inspired black leaders across the globe, and he is considered one of the fathers of Pan-Africanism, the ongoing movement to unite people of African descent in a shared effort to achieve political, economic, and social equality.*

TRADITIONAL STORIES

Common throughout Africa are spider stories, and Liberia is no exception. Ananse (ah-NAN-say) the spider is a clever trickster, but his cleverness often brings about the wrong result, and he usually gets caught in the end. The spider stories found their way into American culture by way of the slaves brought from Africa.

Other stories kept alive in the oral tradition involve legends about ancestors. These stories probably began at the funeral of some great leader, where those present improvised and likely exaggerated stories of battles fought or animals killed. If the stories were good, bits were remembered and repeated at the next celebration, and so on. Proverbs are another part of the oral tradition and are used to pass on the wisdom and values of the tribe.

FILM IN LIBERIA

Liberia has almost no film industry to speak of, and there is only one functioning cinema in the country (the others were destroyed or repurposed during the civil war). Liberians nevertheless enjoy watching movies when they can, and a new organization is catering to those desires. Kriterion Monrovia, founded by a young woman named Pandora Hodge, hosts film screenings around the capital city of Monrovia in an effort to bring film culture to Liberia. Hodge was inspired to launch the project by the dire situation the country found itself in at the end of the civil war. Having fled the fighting as a young child with her family, Hodge was confronted with a postwar world in which there were no jobs and almost no surviving culture. While attending the University of Liberia in 2011, she came up with an idea to address both problems: Kriterion Monrovia would offer work (there are currently eight employees and dozens of volunteers) as well as culture and intellectual debate to the citizens of Monrovia.

Hodge selects films for the traveling cinema to educate viewers, spark discussions, and to make people laugh. Various genres of film are screened, and for many Liberians, Kriterion Monrovia is their first time seeing a movie in a theater-like setting. During the Ebola outbreak, screenings were temporarily halted under the ban on public gatherings, but Hodge used that time to instead travel around the country and warn people about the dangers of the virus; those that were disinclined to heed the government's warnings were far more likely to listen to her, a familiar, trusted face. With the epidemic over, the screenings have resumed, and Kriterion Monrovia is now on the verge of opening an art-house movie theater. Hodge has encouraged Liberians to start making their own films, and she is hopeful that a Liberian film industry will begin to take shape in the next few years.

LIBERIAN MUSIC

Music is an important part of daily life in Liberia and a vibrant expression of Liberian culture. Traditional music has a distinctive sound as a result of the instruments used. Various types of xylophone are common, often with gourds hanging below them to create resonance. Rattles of all kinds—made out of anything from gourds to tin cans—are also used, as well as various stringed instruments, which can include simple lutes, modern acoustic guitars, and everything in between. Bells, clappers, horns, and, of course, drums round out the orchestra.

The most important element of Liberian music is rhythm. Like most other West African music, drums and other percussion instruments are used to set up complex beat patterns, with different rhythms overlaying one another. In tribal society, rhythm is a basic accompaniment to most activities, including rowing boats, sowing seeds, cutting plants, and building houses.

Modern Liberian music has borrowed from this tradition and also from the "highlife" big-band music of Ghana and Sierra Leone, a dance style that emerged in the 1950s that combined African sounds with regimental band music and Latin American rhythms. As soon as recording became possible in Liberia in the 1920s, collections of Liberian music featuring a female Vai singer named Zondogbo became popular. Later, during World War II, Liberian music began to reflect American influences, acquired from the American soldiers stationed in the country. Traditional music was at its most vibrant in the 1960s, when singers such as Zuke Kiazolu and Zina Zaldoa were recorded. Two radio stations, ELBC and ELWA, broadcast popular songs daily and sent researchers out to rural areas to collect new folk songs.

Today, though the Liberian music industry is largely unstructured, the country is producing artists who are making an impact on the international stage. DenG, the first Liberian to be nominated for an MTV Africa Music Award, has collaborated with Nigerian megastar Kcee on his song "Make Dem Talk." F.A. is the first Liberian artist to have a million views on YouTube, and Kanvee Adams, the most successful gospel singer in the country, was the first Liberian to be nominated for a KORA Award (the Pan-African equivalent of a Grammy).

Liberia is also producing entirely new genres of music. The most popular of these is Hipco, which has developed in the streets of Monrovia over the past decade. Hipco takes inspiration from a wide variety of musical styles, ranging from hip-hop and R&B to Nigerian pop and West African dance music, but retains a fresh, upbeat sound all its own. It derives its name from its hip-hop roots as well as the "Colloqua" dialect—the colloquial pidgin English spoken in Monrovia—in which it is performed. Hipco music is often political in nature, and it has an intensely local appeal. The music speaks to the hopes and disappointments of poor, young, urban Liberians, and most successful Hipco artists are themselves from the streets of Monrovia. The most popular Hipco singer, Takun J (whose real name is Jonathan Koffa), was born and raised in the city, and part of his appeal comes from his self-made status—he is a Liberian who achieved success without leaving the country or relying on foreign money.

Takun J has emerged as a musical star in Monrovia, and his brand of uncompromising Hipco has attracted a wide range of listeners.

Takun J's breakthrough came in 2007 with the track "Police Man," in which he spoke out against corrupt local police officers. At a concert soon after, he was arrested by the police, beaten, and only released when an angry crowd threatened to burn down the police station. His most popular album, *My Way*, released in 2012, featured further criticism of corruption and government neglect. The songs on the album were sympathetic to the plight of former child soldiers and victims of sexual abuse, appealing to an entire generation of Liberians who are dealing with these problems. Another song, "They Lie to Us," asks why the schools, roads, and food promised by the government have

Hipco music is so popular in Liberia that at the height of the Ebola crisis, UNICEF teamed up with local musicians, including F.A. and DenG, to produce a track called "Ebola Is Real" to help communicate to skeptical Liberians the severity of the disease. Since native musicians were seen as more trustworthy than foreign doctors, it was thought that the song could reach people who would otherwise dismiss the government's warnings about the virus. Featuring such lyrics as "Ebola is real / It's time to protect yourself," the song instructed people to wash their hands and warned them against burying the bodies of their dead loved ones, all in typical, upbeat Hipco fashion. The song turned out to be a massive hit and was so popular that many Liberians began using it as a ringtone.

never materialized. Takun J has recently converted a courtyard into a bar and performance space where he and other Hipco artists perform, and he is hoping to take his music beyond Liberia's borders.

PICTORIAL AND SCULPTURAL ART

There are many other forms of art in Liberia, foremost among them the elaborate masks that are made for tribal festivals and religious rituals. Although they are considered sacred objects, the masks have been given away to anthropologists—in an effort to preserve them—by tribal leaders who saw their traditions being lost in the move to westernize Liberian society. The masks are made of sapwood and often have steel or aluminum teeth. They are usually brightly painted with dyes collected from indigenous plants and can be beautiful or fierce-looking, depending on their purpose.

Today, replicas of these masks are made for cultural purposes and as craft objects. Liberian craftwork also includes sculpted figures made from a variety of materials. Woodcarvers make figures from ebony, camwood, cherry, walnut, and mahogany; the Kissi carve figures from soapstone; and the Grebo make clay models. The designs for these figures are taken from the totems of indigenous religions. Other craftwork in the country includes woven mats and baskets, cloth, gold and silver jewelry, and musical instruments. Dru, a woodcarver from Liberia, has found fame with exhibitions of his work in the United States.

Among the Americo-Liberian community, painting and sculpture only began in the mid-twentieth century, and the resulting art was largely religious in nature. In the 1960s, a Liberian school of artists emerged, many of them having been trained in Europe, and by the 1970s, regular exhibitions were being held, with galleries displaying the paintings and sculptures of local artists. Many of those artists fled during the civil war, however, and some were killed. The National Museum was looted during the fighting, but a collection of masks and ceramics at Cuttington University remained undisturbed. Painters who have remained in Liberia and survived the fighting include H. Wantue Major, who focuses on graphic images of the horror of war and Naplah E. Naplah, whose paintings depict traditional village life.

Tribal masks such as this one are part of a long tradition in Liberia and serve a spiritual purpose to those who craft them.

INTERNET LINKS

http://www.kriterionmonrovia.org
This is the official website for Kriterion Monrovia, the student-led group seeking to bring film to Liberia and showcase the country's culture.

https://soundcloud.com/takunj
Takun J's SoundCloud page features dozens of songs by the Liberian Hipco artist.

LEISURE

A Liberian man reads a local newspaper at a small restaurant (complete with television) in Monrovia.

BEFORE THE CIVIL WAR DISRUPTED the daily lives of the Liberian people, the country boasted a variety of leisure activities. The cities played host to a variety of nightclubs, discos, restaurants, sporting facilities, and art galleries, many of which were destroyed or shut down during the war.

In rural areas, especially during the long post-harvest period, villagers relaxed through participation in traditional dances and songs during their numerous festivals. These activities were mostly halted by the outbreak of war in 1989 and have only gradually resumed in the years since. The government has been slow to restore electric power to Liberia's cities, and most Liberians are still dealing with grinding poverty and have little time for leisure as a result. As is the case with the arts, government funding for recreational activities has been low; the Johnson Sirleaf administration prioritized other sectors of Liberian society as more in need of investment. Still, sporting events continue to be held in the country; there is an active, free press; and many nightclubs and bars have reopened in Monrovia. For those Liberians seeking relaxation, there are limited, but real, opportunities for leisure in the country.

URBAN RECREATION

Over the last decade, electricity has slowly been restored to Monrovia and the other major cities in Liberia. Since nearly 82 percent of the country's population has no access to electricity at home, the clubs, bars, and

MANCALA

Mancala (man-KAH-lah) is a popular leisure game played throughout the African continent. It is similar to checkers and is played on a boat-shaped wooden board with hollows used to hold stones or other counters. A strategy-based game, the object is to capture more stones than one's opponent. Variations of mancala exist today all over the world.

restaurants that are connected to the electric grid have become the nucleus of urban nightlife. Clubs and discos, some featuring satellite television or live music, pulse with energy and attract the overwhelmingly young Monrovian population. The electricity can be unreliable, however, particularly in smaller towns, so evening diversions are limited to nights when power is available.

There are also cafés (or cookshops, as the residents refer to them) in the city where simple Liberian food can be eaten, as well as more upscale restaurants that attract wealthy Liberians and foreign workers. Churches and tribal associations have their own unique meeting places in the cities, and they often organize group activities. Markets also function as a leisure spot for those who shop for groceries or other goods on a daily basis. In addition to the traditional street-level markets, there are a few Western-style supermarkets in the country, which mainly sell imported foods.

RURAL RECREATION

Until the harvest comes in, most rural Liberians have little opportunity for leisure. When they do get downtime, it is mostly spent at home in the company of their friends and families. In the evenings, rural Liberians relax with a glass of palm wine, followed by a kola nut as a chaser. Pipe smoking is also popular with both men and women. The oral histories and epic tales that are so important to traditional tribal culture play a large part in recreation among rural communities, and even informal family conversations are peppered with stories, proverbs, and cautionary tales. Many rural men plan hunting trips together, not only for food but also to take pleasure in each other's company.

Liberia's national soccer team in 2013.

POPULAR SPORTS

Liberians enjoy watching or participating in several different sports, but none is more beloved than soccer. A national championship is held every year in the country, and Liberia also has a national team organized within the Confederation of African Football (CAF). The Liberian national team has twice qualified for the Africa Cup of Nations but has not made it past the first round. Liberia has never qualified for the World Cup.

The most famous Liberian soccer player is George Weah, who has played in not only his native Liberia but also several European countries. He is a three-time African Player of the Year, a European Player of the Year, and in 1995 he was named the FIFA World Player of the Year. He has since left sports behind and has become a political figure, running for president in 2005 and vice president in 2011. Weah ran for the presidency again in 2017 and won.

Other popular sports in Liberia include basketball, swimming, squash, and track and field, though participation in some of these sports is limited to those wealthy enough to have access to practice facilities. Liberia regularly participates in the Summer Olympics but has no presence at the Winter Olympics. On a more amateur level, schoolchildren enjoy playing kickball, basketball, and soccer.

CHILDREN'S GAMES

Children in Liberia amuse themselves with a multitude of games, many of which involve songs. Among the Gola there is a game called *nenya* (NEN-yah). In this game, a group of children choose one from among them to pretend to be a grain of rice. Another child is assigned to "protect" the grain of rice from the rest of the children, who are all hungry birds. The children must creep into a circle drawn around the "rice" and tag it without being tagged themselves. If tagged, the "bird" becomes the "rice" and the game goes on. As they dart in and out of the circle, the children sing a song that mimics the calls of the birds in the fields.

An all-boys game played by Vai children is *Mba N Ko Dende* (MBAR ehn koh DEN-de), or "Mother Give Me a Canoe." To play, all the children involved hold hands in a circle and choose one boy to be "it." This boy then has to find a weak spot in the chain of hands and break it. As he does so, he sings a song about canoes, asking if he can take the canoe. If a child in the chain answers "yes," the boy who is "it" can try to break his hold. When he succeeds, the next boy enters the circle and the game begins again.

Another popular children's game is one similar to marbles, often played with dried seeds. Four seeds (or marbles, if available) are stacked in a pyramid on the ground, and players flick their own seeds toward it in an effort to knock it down. The first to successfully do so wins.

COMMUNICATIONS AND MEDIA

Communications in Liberia are limited by the lack of electricity in most parts of the country. Landline telephones are rare, and the vast majority of the population uses prepaid cell phones to communicate. The internet is also not in widespread use, as most Liberians have no way to access it. Only about 250,000 Liberians, little more than 5 percent of the population, have internet access.

The media in Liberia consists mostly of radio, television, and print newspapers. Radio is more prevalent than television, as the equipment is easier for Liberians to afford. In addition to the state-run Liberian Broadcasting System (LBS), there are nearly one hundred other local radio stations belonging to private individuals and organizations that broadcast in various parts of the country. Stations from outside the country, including Voice of America and the BBC World Service, can be picked up within Liberia's borders. There are fewer options available to Liberians when it comes to television. Only a handful of stations exist in Monrovia, and most Liberians do not have access to a television.

A FREE PRESS?

In 2010, Liberia established the first freedom of information law in all of West Africa. Despite this, in 2016, two radio stations that had accused President Johnson Sirleaf of corruption were abruptly shut down by the government, ostensibly for a lack of proper permits. The government also moved to silence those who criticized this decision, prompting the international journalistic watchdog organization Reporters Without Borders (RSF) to issue a condemnation of the Johnson Sirleaf administration.

Print newspapers fare much better. There are around a dozen papers that publish regularly, the most prominent among them the *Inquirer*, the *Daily Observer*, the *New Dawn*, and *FrontPageAfrica*. While the freedoms of speech and press are firmly established in Liberia and there is no official government censorship of these papers, the heavy fines associated with the country's libel and slander laws have encouraged Liberian journalists to censor themselves. Journalists that are too critical of the government or expose corruption risk police harassment or lawsuits for slander; if they are unable to pay the often exorbitant fines handed out in these cases, they are jailed. The net effect is therefore a limiting of journalistic freedom, as many media outlets opt not to report on the corruption of government officials, for fear of the legal consequences that will result.

INTERNET LINKS

http://www.fifa.com/associations/association=lbr/index.html
The FIFA profile for the Liberia Football Association features the latest scores from Liberia's national league, as well as news from the world of African soccer.

https://www.liberianobserver.com
The homepage of one of Liberia's largest media outlets, the *Daily Observer*, is one of several sources of the latest news from the country.

FESTIVALS

Liberians celebrate in a wide variety of ways. This woman celebrates her recovery from the Ebola infection.

12

FESTIVALS IN LIBERIA ARE TYPICALLY held to mark important dates in the country's major religions. As with the blending of religions that has taken place in Liberia, festivals have also changed to reflect the different traditions in the country. Christian festivals, for example, have become more energetic and vibrant, adopting propulsive drumming and colorful processions from indigenous religious practices.

Though traditional village celebrations have waned in importance as Christianity and Islam have spread through the country, there are still many song, dance, and performance events that take place among villagers; the Kpelle call these festivals *pelee* (PEL-ee). Secret tribal societies have their own celebrations, usually held when new members are inducted into the group, and there are specific traditions associated with births, weddings, and deaths.

CHRISTIAN AND MUSLIM HOLIDAYS

Liberian Christians celebrate the main Christian festivals, and Christmas and Easter are public holidays in the country. In every small town, Christians celebrate these holidays with a mixture of African and Christian traditions. Indigenous African churches hold lively festivities,

"Celebrating in the counties is a tradition (begun) in 2006. It is intended to take events to the people, to encourage and expand infrastructural development, and to promote national healing and reconciliation." —President Ellen Johnson Sirleaf, marking the country's Independence Day celebrations on July 26, 2014

A shop in Monrovia sells a Christmas tree and other decorations during the Ebola crisis in 2014.

featuring rhythmic music and emotionally charged services involving miraculous events, such as faith healing or speaking in tongues. The Baptists and other older churches are more sedate. At Christmas, church bells are rung and gifts are exchanged. Easter is a more somber occasion, since it marks the crucifixion, resurrection, and eventual ascension of Jesus Christ.

Muslim festivals are not public holidays in Liberia, but they are celebrated throughout the country. Because the Muslim calendar is based on the moon's revolution around Earth rather than Earth's revolution around the sun, the dates of Muslim festivals change every year. Ramadan, the ninth month of the Islamic calendar, is a period of fasting that lasts from dawn to dusk. In the evenings, the fast is broken, and in Muslim areas the cookshops stay open amid an atmosphere of celebration. Eid al-Fitr, the festival that marks the end of Ramadan, begins on the first day of the tenth month and lasts

AFRICA DAY

Africa Day (May 25) celebrates the people and cultures of the African continent. It is celebrated in every African country, as well as among African communities living elsewhere in the world.

for four days. To celebrate, the family home is cleaned, new clothes are bought, families visit one another, and great feasts are held. For Muslims, this marks the successful end of a period of spiritual cleansing and is the most important event of the year. Eid al-Adha, the tenth day of the twelfth month, celebrates Abraham's willingness to sacrifice his son. An animal is slaughtered to commemorate this event, and the meat is given to the poor.

INDIGENOUS AFRICAN CELEBRATIONS

Many indigenous African festivals take place in the fall, after the harvest is gathered and the hard work of the year is over. The Sande and Poro festivals

Liberian Muslims celebrate Eid al-Fitr, the festival that marks the end of the holy month of Ramadan.

CALENDAR OF PUBLIC HOLIDAYS

January 1	*New Year's Day*
February 11	*Armed Forces Day*
Second Wednesday in March	*Decoration Day*
March 15	*J. J. Roberts's Birthday*
April 11	*National Redemption Day*
Second Friday in April	*Prayer and Fast Day*
Variable	*Good Friday*
Variable	*Easter Sunday*
May 14	*National Unification Day*
May 25	*Africa Day*
July 26	*National Independence Day*
First Thursday in November	*Thanksgiving Day*
November 29	*William Tubman's Birthday*
December 25	*Christmas*

often take place at this time, together with the proper celebration of other events, such as funerals, that were delayed until a time when suitable attention could be paid to them.

Among the secret societies, special rituals are performed to mark the passage from childhood to adulthood of the boys and girls of the tribe, and to induct them into the society. Ceremonial masks and costumes, which completely cover the wearer and are kept hidden from outsiders, are worn by the highest-ranking members of the Sande and Poro societies during these rituals. In one Poro ceremony, each boy is enveloped by the masked figure, dressed in a voluminous straw costume; his release signifies a rebirth. Other rituals act out the impaling of the boys, who are believed to then return to their families a different person.

There is joy in some of these celebrations, in the form of dancing, feasting, music, and gifts given to children by their parents. There are also "graduation" festivals, in which boys and girls are allowed to don the traditional tribal

Festivals are often an occasion for bringing professional storytellers into the village for a performance involving music, storytelling, dance, and mime. These stories are often epic poems that exist only in the memories of the storytellers. One well-recorded example of this is a Kpelle myth called the Woi epic, a complicated story about a superhuman hero called Woi who goes on a series of adventures and battles an evil spirit.

The story has no firm beginning or end, and individual episodes are chosen by storytellers that best suit the evening's performance. Many parts of the tale are comic, and current events are often referenced by the storyteller to make the ancient epic more topical. Good storytellers use their bodies and their environment to help tell the tale, sometimes making a shadow play with their arms in the torchlight. The listeners are also encouraged to participate in the epic, either by offering the storyteller pre-planned prompts to keep the story going or by acting as a chorus, singing and playing instruments at appropriate points in the narrative.

garments and, in the case of girls, beads and headdresses. However, it should also be noted that among the rituals performed for most young girls is female genital cutting (FGC), a crude surgical procedure that, unlike the mock impaling of the boys, leaves girls and women with permanent (and in some cases fatal) injuries. This particular practice should under no circumstances be mistaken for a joyous celebration or part of a harmless festival.

BIRTH, MARRIAGE, AND DEATH

Traditional Liberian society contains a number of rituals and ceremonies performed to commemorate births, weddings, and funerals. The most straightforward are performed to celebrate a healthy birth. Since childbirth is still dangerous in much of Liberia, a successful delivery is accompanied by dances and songs to protect the child and its mother. If the child is related to the village chief, the celebrations are even grander. Tribes that have secret societies often have a special house for childbirth, where Sande women assist with the delivery.

City dwellers in Liberia have westernized attitudes toward marriage. They believe in monogamous marriages, and their weddings sometimes include church services. The couple often meets at church or at a dance, and once the decision to marry has been made, they save money for their new home.

Customs in the rural areas are quite different, where women are in some cases considered assets. Marriages are often arranged, and it is legal under customary law to have more than one wife. Most tribal weddings are magnificent affairs, with performances by special dance troupes, a great feast, and gift giving. These ceremonies often end with a procession of the newlyweds and their friends to the groom's village.

Divorce is a relatively straightforward matter that involves arguing in front of the village elders over who gets what; it is not considered shameful in traditional societies. A man or woman who finds out that his or her partner is having an affair can get compensation for the loss of work or possessions

The Tweh farm cemetery in Monrovia is the final resting place for many Liberians.

that this represents. The extramarital relationship is not considered an immoral act, as it might be in Western society, but instead a threat to the economic structure of the family.

Traditional funeral ceremonies, especially among tribes in Sande and Poro societies, often last many days. The body is held for three or four days under the eaves of the palaver hut, and songs and dances are performed around it. Relatives of the deceased then wash the body and bury it themselves. These ceremonies have grown with the spread of Islam and Christianity, and they now often involve Christian hymns or Islamic chants in addition to African songs. During the Ebola outbreak, however, these traditional funeral rites proved disastrous, as the contact between Ebola-infected corpses and healthy relatives often resulted in entire families contracting the disease. Numerous efforts were made to prevent citizens from burying their dead relatives, and eventually a curfew was imposed to cut down on secret, overnight burials. Though the message did eventually reach rural communities, it was only after thousands of Liberians had already lost their lives.

Decoration Day marks the day when people of various religions go to the graveyards to decorate and tidy their family's graves.

INTERNET LINKS

http://www.iexplore.com/articles/travel-guides/africa/liberia/festivals-and-events
This website provides more information about the individual celebrations carried out for particular holidays in Liberia.

http://www.npr.org/sections/goatsandsoda/2014/11/13/363346745/liberians-meet-death-with-flowers-trumpets-and-cameras
This article explores Liberian burial practices and explains why traditional funeral rites contributed to the spread of the Ebola virus.

FOOD

Jollof rice is one of many popular dishes in Liberia.

13

L IBERIAN FOOD HAS SIMILARITIES with other West African cuisines, in which cassava root and rice are the staples of most meals. In Liberia, however, there is also a long tradition of cooking brought to the country by Americo-Liberians and other Western expatriates. Food is difficult for many Liberians to come by, so even the simplest meals are immensely important, and special recipes are often a part of Liberian festivals and celebrations.

"Hearty, spicy and influenced by the immigrants and settlers who have over the years made this tiny coastal country home, (Liberian food) incorporates the best of West African cooking with traditions from the American South." —Helene Cooper, journalist and White House correspondent for the *New York Times*

BASIC INGREDIENTS

Grains, fruits, and vegetables form the staples of the Liberian diet. Both types of rice, wet and dry, can be grown in the country without the complex irrigation systems that are used elsewhere in the world. Rice is grown in almost every rural household and is sold in the city markets. Cassava is also commonly grown. An edible root that has few nutrients, cassava thrives in the damp climate of Liberia and can be left in the ground until it is needed. The traditional preparation of cassava roots involves soaking them in water for several days to ferment before cooking. Other starchy foods grown in the country include *eddoes* (taro, an edible root), plantains, sweet corn, and sweet potatoes.

Liberia also has many types of fresh produce. A wide variety of vegetables are grown in kitchen gardens, including cucumbers, okra, collard greens, lima beans, cabbages, onions, and eggplants. The leaves of sweet potato and cassava plants are also boiled and eaten as vegetables. Fruit is plentiful and includes soursop, grapefruit, mangoes, oranges, pineapples, bananas, watermelons, and coconuts.

Cassava roots and leaves form the basis for many meals in Liberia, and are a dietary staple for most Liberians.

Kola trees are cultivated in kitchen gardens as well. Though the kola nut has little nutritional value, it does contain caffeine and is therefore chewed as a stimulant. Other nuts common to Liberian cuisine include peanuts, which are used in cakes, cookies, and sauces, and palm nuts, the pulp of which is an important dietary staple.

PROTEIN

Meat is not readily available in Liberian villages, and hunting and fishing remain the primary sources of supply. Game includes antelope and wild pigs, as well as more exotic animals, including leopards, lizards, snakes, and frogs. Women and children help collect fish, usually together. The children will enter a river and splash about. This will frighten the fish into swimming downstream and into the nets held by their mothers. Livestock is raised, but not in quantities high enough to meet the needs of the entire population. Chickens are usually saved for their eggs, and cattle are considered a luxury and only slaughtered on special occasions. Goat is a popular meat in the cities and is used in a number of dishes.

Another method of fishing involves poisoning a pool of water with bark from the sasswood tree. This stuns the fish, making them easy to collect, without making them poisonous to eat.

LIBERIAN MEALS

A typical Liberian meal usually consists of boiled rice covered with a spicy sauce that may or may not contain meat. Sometimes, a kind of risotto called *jollof* (JOH-lof) is made with rice, meat, and vegetables. A seasonal alternative to rice is cassava, cooked into a porridge with other vegetables and meat or made into boat-shaped cakes that are used to scoop up an accompanying stew.

Women work together to make *fufu*, a constant presence in Liberian feasts.

Other common dishes include *fufu* (FOO-foo), a fermented cassava porridge, and *dumboy* (DUM-boy), the unfermented version. These are served with palm butter, a stew that often contains meat, beans, onions, or vegetables. *Tumborgee* (tum-BOR-gee), or fermented palm butter, is readily available in Lofa County. Frog soup is another common dish, and deep-fried vegetables and fish are popular.

In a Liberian feast, all the dishes are set out together—nothing is cleared away during the meal, and no new dishes are brought in. *Dumboy* and *fufu* form the base of the meal and are served with palm butter, palaver sauce (a meat stew made with spinach leaves), or *tumborgee*. Goat soup and "check rice" (rice and okra) are also served. Meat dishes can include pig's trotter (the cooked foot of a pig) with cabbage, fish with sweet potato leaves, or shrimp with palm nuts. Fried plantains and organ soup, the national dishes, are also likely to be present. Desserts can range from fruit and cakes to rice bread or sweet potato pone. In a village feast, utensils consist of spoons, bowls, and plates. In a city feast, there are Western utensils, glasses, and a place setting for each guest.

RESTAURANTS

The most common kind of dining establishment in Liberia is the cookshop, a small restaurant that serves simple cuisine. Country chop, the most famous

Popular drinks in Liberia include bottled beer brewed in Monrovia, palm wine made from fermented palm fruit, ginger beer, and rum derived from sugarcane. Milk is rarely drunk, and coffee is only popular in the larger towns and cities.

Palm wine is made by collecting the sap from palm trees in a calabash—a hollowed-out gourd hardened in the sun—where natural yeasts collect on it. Fermentation is rapid. At first sweet and fizzy, the drink quickly turns alcoholic, and in two weeks it becomes a sour wine. Palm wine is an essential part of rural celebrations and public meetings, and can even be used as currency. A kola nut is often sucked while palm wine is drunk, since kola acts as a stimulant and is said to combat the effects of the wine.

dish at these cookshops, consists of meat, fish, and greens fried in palm oil. In addition to the cookshops, the city of Monrovia features a range of dining establishments, from street stalls selling deep-fried foods to gourmet restaurants serving French or Italian cuisine. American-style restaurants serve hamburgers, fried chicken, and American breakfasts alongside traditional Liberian dishes, while Lebanese restaurants sell hummus, *fuul* (FU-ul, a salad made of beans and olive oil), *khobez* (KOH-bez, Lebanese bread), and baklava. Another import from the West is the many pastry shops that sell cookies, cakes, chocolate, and ice cream. Many local ice creams are available, as well as Monrovian coconut pie, a dessert made with grated coconut meat, milk, and eggs.

COOKING EQUIPMENT

In the villages, the basic means of cooking is an outdoor open fire at the rear of the home. A hearth is made from three flat stones, and a fire is lit in the center. A large iron cooking pot rests on the stones, and locally made wooden utensils are used to stir food. Covers for food are woven from palm fiber or, in the bigger towns, made of plastic. Fishing nets, another vital piece of equipment, are also made from palm fiber. Plastic buckets and enamel bowls are often part of a dowry, and the iron cooking pot is an object of great value. Every piece of kitchen equipment is treasured, and very few things are thrown away. Empty produce cans are reused as cooking pots, and glass jars are a rare luxury.

At mealtime, most people eat with either their hands or a carved wooden spoon. The bowls into which food is distributed are usually wooden as well, though plastic or enamel bowls purchased from a market have grown more common.

In the cities, the degree of sophistication of the kitchen varies enormously. The wealthiest Liberians have modern gas stoves and refrigerators, while most citizens rely on charcoal fires built in small, open-roofed huts outside of their homes. A butane gas cylinder is a sign of a well-to-do family, as are drinking glasses, factory-made plates, and metal knives and forks.

Bugabug, or termites, are eaten either raw or roasted in Liberia.

INTERNET LINKS

http://www.libfood.com
Based in Atlanta, Georgia, LIBFOOD is a mail-order service that will deliver traditionally prepared Liberian cuisine to any location in the United States.

http://www.nytimes.com/2010/06/20/travel/20PersonalJourney.html?mcubz=0
Liberian food and dining practices are discussed in this article.

JOLLOF RICE

1 pound boneless chicken
½ pound beef cubes
½ pound bacon
Salt, black pepper, and flour, as needed
½ cup oil or shortening
2 onions, sliced
1 pepper, sliced
3 ounces tomato paste
1½ pounds cabbage, cut into chunks
1½ cups rice
6 cups water

DIRECTIONS

1. Cut chicken, beef, and bacon into ½-inch chunks. Sprinkle with salt and pepper to taste, and coat with flour.
2. Heat oil in a frying pan, add the meat in small batches, and brown the meat. Remove the meat, setting it aside in a bowl.
3. Sauté the onions and pepper in the oil in pot until soft, about 5 minutes.
4. Return the meat to the pot and add the tomato paste.
5. Add water, cover, and heat to boiling. Lower heat and simmer for 10 minutes.
6. Add rice, bring to a boil. Reduce heat.
7. Add cabbage and simmer, stirring often, for 20 minutes.
8. Serve while hot.

SWEET POTATO PONE

1 to 2 cups flour
1½ teaspoons baking powder
½ teaspoon salt
¼ teaspoon ground cloves
¼ teaspoon cinnamon
¼ teaspoon nutmeg
2 eggs, slightly beaten
2 cups sweet potatoes, mashed
   and chilled
Oil for deep-frying

DIRECTIONS
1. Combine flour, baking powder, salt, cloves, cinnamon, and nutmeg in a bowl and stir well to combine.
2. In another large mixing bowl, beat the eggs and sweet potatoes together.
3. Add the dry mixture to the wet mixture until a stiff dough is formed.
4. Roll out dough on a lightly floured surface to ½-inch thickness and cut into shapes.
5. Heat about 1 inch of oil in a deep saucepan. Fry dough in batches for about 4 minutes.
6. Drain, cool, dust with powdered sugar (optional), and serve.

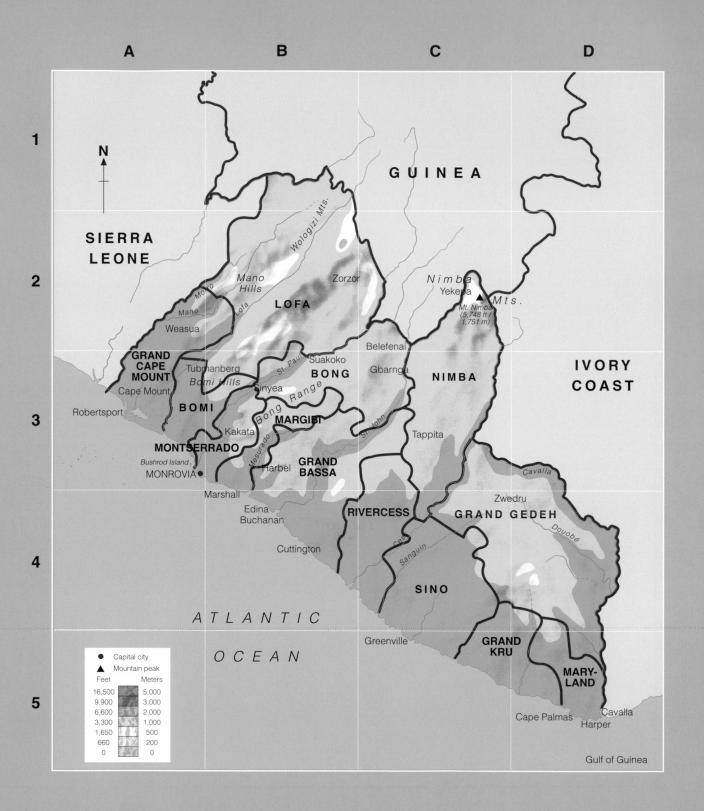

A B C D

1

N

GUINEA

SIERRA
LEONE

2

Wologizi Mts.

*Mano
Hills*

Zorzor

Nimba

Yekepa

Mts.

*Mt. Nimba
(5,748 ft /
1,751 m)*

LOFA

Mano

Moro

Lofa

Weasua

Belefenai

GRAND
CAPE
MOUNT

Tubmanberg

Bomi Hills

Suakoko

BONG

Gbarnga

NIMBA

IVORY
COAST

Cape Mount

Sinyea

St. Paul

Robertsport

BOMI

Bong Range

3

Kakata

MARGIBI

St. John

Tappita

MONTSERRADO

Masurado

Harbel

GRAND
BASSA

Bushrod Island

MONROVIA

Cavalla

Marshall

Zwedru

Edina
Buchanan

RIVERCESS

GRAND GEDEH

Douobé

Cuttington

Cess

Sanguin

4

SINO

ATLANTIC

OCEAN

Greenville

GRAND
KRU

MARY-
LAND

● Capital city

▲ Mountain peak

Feet		Meters
16,500		5,000
9,900		3,000
6,600		2,000
3,300		1,000
1,650		500
660		200
0		0

Cape Palmas

Harper

Cavalla

Gulf of Guinea

5

MAP OF LIBERIA

Atlantic Ocean, A3—A5, B3—B5, C4—C5, D5

Belefenai, C2
Bomi, A3, B3
Bomi Hills, A3, B3
Bong, B2—B3, C2—C3
Bong Range, B3
Buchanan, B4
Bushrod Island, A3

Cape Mount, A3
Cape Palmas, D5
Cavalla, D5
Cavalla River, C3, D3—D5
Cess River, B4, C4
Cuttington, B4

Douobé River, D4

Edina, B4

Gbarnga, C3
Grand Bassa, B3—B4, C3—C4
Grand Cape Mount, A2—A3, B2
Grand Gedeh, C3—C4, D3—D5
Grand Kru, C4—C5, D4—D5
Greenville, C5
Guinea, C1
Gulf of Guinea, D5

Harbel, B3
Harper, D5

Ivory Coast, C2—C3, D1—D5

Kakata, B3

Lofa, A2—A3, B1—B3, C2
Lofa River, B1—B3, C1

Mano Hills, B2
Mano River, A2, B1—B2
Margibi, B3—B4
Marshall, B4
Maryland, D4—D5
Mesurado River, B3
Monrovia, A3
Montserrado, A3, B3
Morro River, A2—A3, B1—B2
Mount Nimba, C2

Nimba, C2—C4
Nimba Mountains, C2

Rivercess, B4, C3—C4
Robertsport, A3

Saint John River, B3—B4, C2—C3
Saint Paul River, A3, B3
Sanguin River, C4
Sierra Leone, A1—A3, B1—B2

Sino, C4
Sinyea, B3
Suakoko, B3

Tappita, C3
Tubmanberg, A3

Weasua, A2
Wologizi Mountains, B1—B2

Yekepa, C2

Zorzor, C2
Zwedru, D4

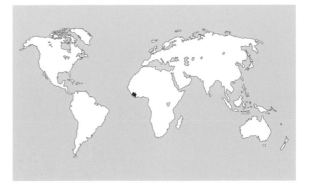

ECONOMIC LIBERIA

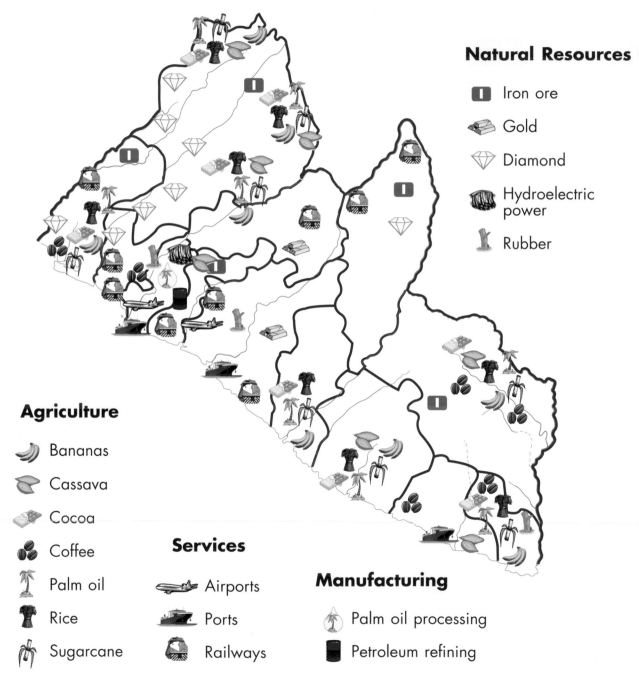

Natural Resources

- Iron ore
- Gold
- Diamond
- Hydroelectric power
- Rubber

Agriculture

- Bananas
- Cassava
- Cocoa
- Coffee
- Palm oil
- Rice
- Sugarcane

Services

- Airports
- Ports
- Railways

Manufacturing

- Palm oil processing
- Petroleum refining

OVERVIEW

Despite the country's rich natural resources, a fourteen-year civil war and the 2014—2015 Ebola epidemic have left Liberia's economy in a very fragile state. Growth in the economy was near zero between 2014 and 2016, and the majority of the Liberian population makes less than one US dollar per day. Ellen Johnson Sirleaf's administration succeeded in bringing foreign investment back into Liberia and was also responsible for working out a deal to forgive much of the country's debt. Still, Liberia is heavily dependent on foreign aid, and much of the nation's infrastructure remains either damaged or destroyed years after the civil war came to an end. With the Ebola crisis over, investments in the country's health-care, education, transportation, and sanitation sectors are needed to boost the quality of life of the Liberian people, thereby growing the economy in the long run.

GROSS DOMESTIC PRODUCT (GDP)
$2.112 billion (US; 2016 estimate)

GDP PER CAPITA
$900 (US; 2016 estimate)

GROWTH RATE
0 percent, as a result of the Ebola epidemic in 2014

GDP BY SECTOR
Agriculture: 44.7 percent
Industry: 6.8 percent
Services: 48.5 percent

CURRENCY
1 US dollar = 92.33 Liberian dollars
(2016 estimate)

UNEMPLOYMENT RATE
2.8 percent (2014 estimate)

MAIN PRODUCTS
Bananas, cassava, cocoa, coffee, rice, palm oil, sugarcane, sheep, goats, diamonds, gold, iron ore, rubber, timber

LABOR FORCE BY OCCUPATION
Agriculture: 70 percent
Industry and manufacturing: 8 percent
Services: 22 percent

MAIN EXPORTS
Rubber, timber, iron ore, diamonds, cocoa, coffee

MAIN TRADE PARTNERS
Exports: Poland, China, India, United States, Greece (2015 estimate)
Imports: Singapore, China, South Korea, Japan, Philippines (2015 estimate)

CULTURAL LIBERIA

Providence Island
This small offshore island has a bandstand and an amphitheater where performances of traditional African music and dance are staged.

The National Cultural Center
Located in Kendeja, this center is a showcase for the tribal life, customs, and traditions of Liberia. Representatives of the sixteen tribes live and work in harmony, practicing and helping one another improve their music, dances, and arts and crafts.

Liberian Music
Since peace has returned to Liberia, local music, such as West African Highlife music, is played in the bars and clubs of Monrovia, especially around Gurley Street.

Monrovian Markets
In the waterfront markets of the capital, all sorts of Liberian handicrafts are traded, including carvings in sapwood, camwood, ebony, and mahogany; stone items; soapstone carvings; ritual masks; metal jewelry and figurines; and reed dolls.

Silver Beach
Just south of Monrovia, this beautiful beach is popular as a local getaway for Monrovians.

Traditional Artifacts
Before the civil war, the National Museum of Liberia, located in the Supreme Court building in Monrovia, was home to masks and ceramic objects. Some of these have been salvaged and are now housed at Cuttington University College in Suakoko.

Firestone Plantation
As the world's largest single rubber plantation, the Firestone Plantation at Harbel has to be seen to be believed. Today it operates at much-reduced capacity.

Sapo National Park
Sapo National Park in Sino County is Liberia's largest protected area of rain forest and the only national park. It contains the second-largest tropical rain forest in West Africa, after Taï National Park in neighboring Ivory Coast. Recently designated a conservation area, the national park is a haven for West African flora and fauna, including rare animal species, such as the pygmy hippo, Liberian mongoose, chimpanzee, and Jentink's duiker.

ABOUT THE CULTURE

OFFICIAL NAME
Republic of Liberia

NATIONALITY
Liberian

FLAG DESCRIPTION
Eleven equal horizontal stripes of red alternating with white, with a white five-pointed star on a blue square in the upper left corner. The design is based closely on the US flag.

CAPITAL
Monrovia

LAND AREA
37,189 square miles (96,320 sq km)

MAJOR TOWNS
Gbarnga, Buchanan, Ganta, Kakata, Zwedru, Harbel, Harper

POPULATION
4.3 million (2016)

BIRTHRATE
33.9 per 1,000 population (2016)

DEATH RATE
9.5 per 1,000 population (2016)

POPULATION GROWTH RATE
2.44 percent (2016)

LIFE EXPECTANCY
Total population: 59 years
Male: 57.3 years
Female: 60.8 years (2016 estimate)

ADMINISTRATIVE DISTRICTS (COUNTIES)
Bomi, Bong, Gbarpolu, Grand Bassa, Grand Cape Mount, Grand Gedeh, Grand Kru, Lofa, Margibi, Maryland, Montserrado, Nimba, River Cess, River Gee, Sinoe

HIGHEST POINT
Mount Wuteve (4,747 feet/1,447 m)

HEAD OF STATE
President George Weah

MAJOR RIVERS
Saint Paul, Lofa

LANGUAGES
English, plus twenty or more indigenous languages

RELIGIONS
Christianity (85.6 percent),
Islam (12.2 percent),
traditional animist religions (0.6 percent),
other (0.2 percent)

TRIBES
Bassa, Belleh, Dei, Gbandi, Gio, Gola, Grebo, Kissi, Kpelle, Krahn, Kru, Loma, Mandingo, Mano, Mende, Vai

TIMELINE

IN LIBERIA	IN THE WORLD

1460s
Portuguese traders arrive along the
Grain Coast (now Liberia).

1776
US Declaration of Independence is signed.

1808
The slave trade is formally outlawed in the United
States. Colonization efforts gain popularity.

1822
The American Colonization Society begins
the process of helping freed slaves return to Africa.
The first group of colonists lands at
Cape Mesurado and founds Monrovia.

1824
The colonists adopt the name of
Liberia for their new country.

1847
A constitution modeled on that of the
United States is drawn up. Liberia is the first
African colony to become an independent state.

1884–1885
The Berlin Conference divides the African continent
among the European powers. This prompts the
Liberian government to gain greater control over the
interior of the country and its indigenous population.

1914–1918
World War I.

1939–1945
World War II. Liberia signs a defense agreement with
the Allies during the war.

1943
William Tubman is elected president of Liberia.

1945
The Cold War begins. Liberia becomes the most
important American ally and military staging area
on the African continent.

1951
Women and property owners vote in the
presidential election for the first time.

1971
William Tubman dies and is
succeeded by William Tolbert

1980
Master Sergeant Samuel Doe stages a
military coup and Tolbert is assassinated.
A People's Redemption Council headed by Doe
suspends the constitution and takes power.

1985
Doe wins election amid widespread
accusations of vote rigging.

IN LIBERIA	IN THE WORLD

1989
The National Patriotic Front of Liberia (NPFL), led by Charles Taylor, begins an uprising against the government.

1990
Doe is executed by a splinter group of the NPFL led by Prince Johnson.

1991
Breakup of the Soviet Union. The Cold War ends.

1991–2002
Civil war rages in Sierra Leone. Charles Taylor abets the rebels.

1997
A peace accord leads to a cease-fire in the civil war. Charles Taylor wins a landslide victory in presidential elections.

1999
Ghana and Nigeria accuse Liberia of supporting Revolutionary United Front rebels in Sierra Leone. Charles Taylor's government fails to bring stability to the country. The civil war resumes.

2001
Terrorists crash planes in New York, Washington, DC, and Pennsylvania. The United States launches the War on Terror.

2003
Peace talks begin to end the civil war. President Taylor is accused of war crimes, leaves the country. The interim government and rebels sign a peace accord.

2006
Ellen Johnson Sirleaf takes office as the first female president of Liberia in January.

2007
Former president Charles Taylor is formally put on trial for war crimes in the Netherlands.

2008
Economic recession hits the United States and Europe, affecting markets worldwide.

2011
Ellen Johnson Sirleaf and Leymah Gbowee receive the Nobel Peace Prize; Johnson Sirleaf is reelected president.

2014
An outbreak of the Ebola virus in West Africa becomes an epidemic when it reaches Monrovia.

2014
Scottish voters reject a split from the United Kingdom.

2016
Liberia is declared free of Ebola.

2016
Donald Trump is elected president of the United States.

2017
Presidential elections are held to determine Ellen Johnson Sirleaf's successor.

GLOSSARY

Aladura
An African Christian church.

Americo-Liberian
Liberians of African American descent.
These people can trace their ancestry to the
free blacks and former slaves who settled in
Liberia in the nineteenth century.

Ananse
A spider that figures in African stories.

calabash
A container made from a hollowed gourd.

colonization
A movement of the late eighteenth and
early nineteenth centuries that sought to
establish colonies in Africa for former slaves
and free blacks.

Congo
People descended from slaves rescued from
slave ships in the Atlantic Ocean.

Creole
A language that amalgamates two others.

dumboy (**DUM-boy**)
Unfermented cassava porridge.

fufu (**FOO-foo**)
Fermented cassava porridge.

kwi (**KWEE**)
Pidgin English for "foreigner."

Malinke
The language spoken by the Mandingo.

mancala (man-KAH-lah)
A board game played with counters.

nenya (**NEN-yah**)
Gola children's game.

palaver hut
A place where village councils meet.

pelee (**PEL-ee**)
Music, dance, and performance festival.

pone (**POH-ney**)
A popular dish in Liberia; in this book, it is
made with sweet potatoes, but often times
pone is corn based.

Poro
A male secret society.

Sande
A female secret society.

syllabary
A kind of alphabet consisting of a character
for each combination of vowel and
consonant, or syllable.

tumborgee (**tum-BOR-gee**)
Fermented palm butter.

zoe (**ZOH**)
A priest, usually the head of Poro or
Sande society.

FOR FURTHER INFORMATION

BOOKS

Baughan, Brian. *Liberia*. The Evolution of Africa's Major Nations. Broomall, PA: Mason Crest Publishers, 2014.

Gay, John. *Red Dust on the Green Leaves: A Kpelle Twins' Childhood*. Thompson, CT: InterCulture Associates, 1973.

Gbowee, Leymah, and Carol Mithers. *Mighty Be Our Powers: How Sisterhood, Prayer, and Sex Changed a Nation at War*. New York: Hachette Book Group, 2011.

Miller, Debra A. *Liberia*. Modern Nations of the World. San Diego: Lucent Books, 2004.

Olukoju, Ayodeji Oladimeji. *Culture and Customs of Liberia*. Culture and Customs of Africa. Westport, CT: Greenwood Press, 2006.

Sirleaf, Ellen Johnson. *This Child Will Be Great: Memoir of a Remarkable Life by Africa's First Woman President*. New York: HarperCollins, 2009.

Streissguth, Thomas. *Liberia in Pictures*. Visual Geography. Minneapolis, MN: Lerner Publishing Group, 2006.

Van der Kraaij, Fred. *Liberia: From the Love of Liberty to Paradise Lost*. Leiden, Netherlands: African Studies Centre, 2015.

WEBSITES

http://www.allafrica.com/liberia

https://www.cia.gov/library/publications/the-world-factbook/geos/li.html

http://www.frontpageafricaonline.com

http://www.iucn.org

http://www.liberianforum.com/news.htm

http://www.unicef.org/infobycountry/liberia.html

FILMS

Siatta Scott Johnson and Daniel Junge (Dir.). *Iron Ladies of Liberia, 2007.*

Jonathan Stack and James Brabazon (Dir.). *Liberia: An Uncivil War, 2004.*

MUSIC

Arthur Alberts. *Songs of the African Coast: Cafe Music of Liberia*. Yarngo, LLC, 2007.

George Weah, Epee, and Koum. *Lone Star Liberia*. Sonodisc, 1999.

Liberia: The Music of Vai Islam. Multicultural Media, 2007.

Takun J. *My Way*. Jazzo Entertainment, 2012.

BIBLIOGRAPHY

Boe, P. Nathaniel. *Miracle on the Atlantic Coast: How to Transform Liberia into a Peaceful and Prosperous Country*. Bloomington, IN: AuthorHouse, 2007.

Boone, Clinton C. *Liberia as I Know It*. Southfield, MI: Written Images, 2006.

Brown, Robert. *The Novels of Wilton Sankawulo: A Critical Study*. Bloomington, IN: AuthorHouse, 2014.

Epstein, Helen. "Ebola in Liberia: An Epidemic of Rumors." *New York Review of Books*, December 18, 2014. http://www.nybooks.com/articles/2014/12/18/ebola-liberia-epidemic-rumors.

Greene, Graham. *Journey Without Maps*. London: Penguin Classics, 2006.

Horace, Selena Gennehma. *African Recipes: The Liberian Cuisine*. Washington, DC: Horasel Productions, 2003.

McPherson, J. H. T. *History of Liberia*. Kila, MT: Kessinger Publishing Co., 2004.

Meadows, David E. *Liberia*. New York: Berkley Books, 2003.

Moran, Mary H. *Liberia: The Violence of Democracy*. Philadelphia: University of Pennsylvania Press, 2006.

Parshley, Lois. "After Ebola." *Atlantic*, July/August 2016. https://www.theatlantic.com/magazine/archive/2016/07/after-ebola/485609.

Sankawulo, Wilton. *Sundown at Dawn: A Liberian Odyssey*. Houston: Dusty Spark Publishing, 2005.

Watkins, Samuel R. *Liberia Communication*. Bloomington, IN: AuthorHouse, 2007.

INDEX

143

INDEX